NIrV
kid
REFERENCE
LIBRARY

Kid ATLAS

Important Places in the Bible

AND

Where to Find Them

Written by
Ruth van der Maas, Marnie Wooding,
and Rick Osborne

Zonderkidz

Departure

Are you ready to go on a road trip through time and space? Ready to explore the world as it was, as it is now, and as it will be in the future? From day one of God's creation, the world has been constantly changing.

Ever since Adam and Eve packed their bags and left the Garden of Eden, people have been on the move, building roads, cities, and countries all over the place. Then every few hundred years, we change them all over again. We're still doing it!

We may change how we do things and our planet may change how it looks, but God is always the same, and he has a great plan for each one of us. To know where we are in God's plan, we have to look at the past and see where we've been. The past is a blast if you know where to go, what to look for, and what to do.

Remember that Bible events, like when Jesus walked on water or Moses went toe-to-toe with Pharaoh, actually happened in real places. So let's explore what happened, where it happened, and how that spot has changed over the thousands of years from then until now.

Kidatlas provides the maps and the ticket to some of the most interesting stops around the globe. So step right up and take a seat. We're wasting time. And time, my friend, is a terrible thing to waste!

Mount of Olives

Mount Sinai

Sea of Galilee

Damascus

The first rule of geographical touring is that you don't really appreciate a good map until you're lost in the middle of a scorpion-infested desert … and you're running low on gas. Okay, that's a worst-case scenario. But maps are important. Maps put you in the driver's seat with information at your fingertips.

A map is simply a drawing of a place—usually from a bird's-eye view. You know … from above. Try this: Ask your folks to put a stepladder in your room. Climb to the top and draw what you can see from above. Draw the top of your desk, bed, laundry hamper, and fishbowl (if you have fish). There, you just did a map of the stuff in your room. Show it to anybody, and they'll know just where to find your desk, bed, and laundry hamper (although your dirty socks wouldn't be the best tourist stop).

Get a map of your town and unfold it. (Got it?) See if you can find your street! What you're looking at is called a road map. Maps come in every size, shape, and subject.

People use maps all the time for different things. If you want to know about something, there's probably a map that will tell you— from weather maps, to maps of the ocean, to three-dimensional relief maps that are models of mountains and other cool stuff.

When you put all kinds of maps together in one super-heavy enormous book, you call that book an atlas. Why atlas? Well, a long time ago, these people called the Greeks (Greeks, not geeks) told a story about this really strong guy named Atlas. He was supposed to carry the entire world on his shoulders. You can have the world right where you want it, too, when you carry an atlas with all kinds of maps. This atlas is stuffed full of maps that tell God's history—the what, where, and when of the Bible.

Maps were easy to make when everybody thought the world was flat. But when we discovered the earth was round … hmmm, that was a problem. Try gift-wrapping a basketball. How can you show both sides of a round earth on a flat map? No problemo! Imagine peeling an orange. For a flat world map, we sort of peel the surface of the earth off. Then we stretch it flat, and before you can say "cartography" (map making), we have our modern-day world map, showing both sides, or as we in the map biz say, the northern and southern hemispheres of the earth.

Before God created the world, he created something a little bigger to put our world in. How much bigger? Let's check it out!

- Did you know the first maps drawn thousands of years ago showed hunting and fishing spots?

- What's the difference between maps and charts? Maps show the land and charts show the sea.

DID YOU KNOW

The first stop we want to make is a big one. How big? Gigantic universe big! God created the entire universe and filled it with everything from super galaxies to microscopic solar dust. Our planet Earth is an important part of this very big picture, even though we are just one small planet in an endless outer space. If you want to find Earth on our solar system map, it's the third planet from the sun. But remember, we are just one planet in one solar system in the Milky Way galaxy. The universe is full of millions of galaxies.

How big exactly is the universe? Well, people have been observing space for thousands of years. Just to reach the farthest part of the universe that we have seen with our super technological telescopes would take a long time. How long? Traveling 186,300 miles per second (the speed that light travels), it would take 6,000 million years to reach the farthest part of the universe.

Big universe = a very big God. That's right. God created it all, and he understands how everything works—from the life-giving heat the sun gives off to the way our planet spins to give us day and night. It all works together just right so that we can live here on Earth. That's exactly why God created the universe! He loves us and wanted to give us the best place to live in all the … well … universe.

Hot Vacation Spot!

The sun is one huge ball of gas 865,000 miles in diameter. The visible surface of the sun is a stormy layer of gas about 186 miles deep. Pack your sunscreen, because the temperature of the core of the sun is only about 29 million degrees Fahrenheit or 12 million degrees Celsius. The sun has nine planets that orbit around it: Mercury, Venus, Earth, Mars, Jupiter, Saturn, Uranus, Neptune, and Pluto.

- When you watch the night sky, you can see only about 2,000 stars at any one time out of the 100,000 million or so stars in our galaxy.

- If the planet Pluto suddenly exploded into nothingness, it would take that fiery image five and a half hours traveling at light speed before we saw it back here on Earth.

- Did you know that the way Earth was built and its position in our solar system makes it the only planet with exactly the right conditions to support life?

Now let's take a look at the beginning of our amazing planet called Earth. After two days of work, God got the universe spinning in all the right directions. He then spent the next four days creating the oceans, the land, plants, fish, birds, land animals, and changing seasons. Some people believe that God's days were twenty-four hours long, but others believe they were longer periods of time. When everything was ready, God made his greatest creation—the first two people on earth—Adam and Eve. God put them in charge of the Earth and gave them the Garden of Eden to live in.

Possible Locations for the Garden of Eden

▲ Mt. Ararat

Euphrates River

Tigris River

GARDEN OF EDEN

THE GREAT SEA (MEDITERRANEAN SEA)

Babel? (later the site of Babylon)

Next Stop – A Garden Party

The location of the Garden of Eden has puzzled researchers for hundreds of years. We do have some clues in the Bible. A large river flowed through Eden that eventually split into four smaller rivers. The Bible says that two of these rivers were called the Tigris and Euphrates. That's a great clue! To stand on the banks of these two rivers today, you have to travel to a country called Iraq in Western Asia. The Euphrates is a big-time river at 1,700 miles long. The Tigris is smaller at 1,150 miles. Researchers have narrowed their search for Eden to two places along these rivers.

One suggested spot for the Garden of Eden is where the Euphrates empties into the ocean at the Persian Gulf. The other is somewhere near the beginning of these rivers in the highlands. But still other researchers think the Garden was destroyed by Noah's great flood and will never be found. So although we know what part of the world the Garden was in, the exact spot is still a mystery.

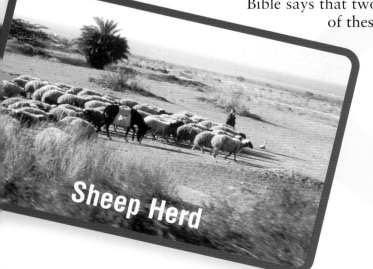

Sheep Herd

But here are some interesting things to think about. Archaeologists have discovered the earliest signs of animals being used and cared for by people near these rivers. They believe that wild sheep were herded there. That same area between the two rivers would later prove to be one of the first and best places for farming in the ancient world! So amazing things were happening there at a very early time. Was the area around the Tigris and Euphrates Rivers the place Adam and Eve first called home? We'll leave that for you to decide.

Hey, What About Those Dinosaurs?

Genesis 1:21 says that God created great sea creatures, and some Bible researchers believe that dinosaurs and people lived together before the Flood. They say that the behemoth and leviathan (mentioned in Job 40–41) are dinosaurs. Other Christians think these "terrible lizards" lived long before God created people. So what happened to our ferocious friends?

Were they wiped out in Noah's Flood, or did they become toast long before that when a huge meteorite hit the Earth? You decide. But know this: no matter when dinosaurs lived or how they died, we know for sure that God created everything, including dinosaurs. He created all animals as separate kinds, and no animals evolved from dinosaurs.

End of Eden

Then Satan tempted Eve and Adam, and they ate from the Tree of Knowledge of Good and Evil. Their sin separated them from God, and he sent them from the garden (their home with God) into the world. All of their children would now be born with sin and separated from God as well, and so would their

joke

What is as large as a dinosaur but weighs nothing?

A dinosaur's shadow.

children and so on all the way to us. The world would never be the same. Adam and Eve's choice to do things their own way—not God's way—affected us all! But never fear, God had a plan (more on that later).

Life became very hard outside of God's garden. People worked long days farming and herding animals. Adam and Eve's children and grandchildren soon traveled to all parts of the world.

- About three hundred varieties of dinosaurs have been discovered so far.

- No one knows what language Adam and Eve spoke, but some of the world's oldest written languages were discovered in the area of the Garden of Eden.

DID YOU KNOW?

Well over a thousand years and many offspring after Adam was created, along came a guy named Noah. By then had everyone learned a thing or two about how bad sinning was? Nope! Sin had only grown bigger! People were still doing their own thing and ignoring God's will.

Everybody, that is, except good old Noah and his family. They were doing things God's way! And that's a very good thing. You might remember Noah … he built an ark (ship) and took one of the most important cruises in history. God instructed him to take some of every type of animal into the ark: seven each of "clean" animals and two each of "unclean" animals. (See Genesis 7:1-3.) Then God destroyed all the wicked people in the world by sending a flood. The flood lasted for forty days and nights. But the total time spent on the ark was 371 days—more than a year. That's a lot of time to spend with a bunch of animals! How many animals went on the ark? Bible researchers estimate between two thousand to fifty thousand animals. Phew, talk about zoo keeping! Some researchers think some of the animals went into hibernation (a natural long sleep) during the trip.

The ark was one mighty impressive ship! It was big! It was 450 feet long, 75 feet

joke

What doesn't get wetter no matter how much it rains?

The ocean!

wide, and 45 feet high. It had windows, decks, and separate areas for the different animals.

First Stop: Mount Ararat

The Bible tells us that when the floodwaters finally began to disappear, the ark drifted until it beached on top of one of the mountains—Ararat. Mount Ararat is a far-off

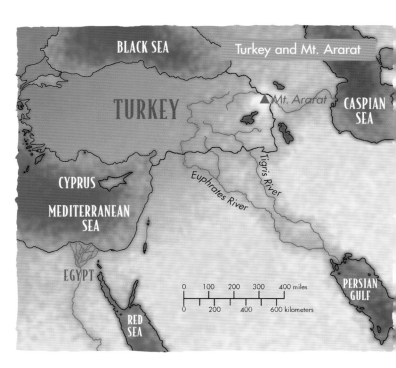

lonely mountain in the high plains of eastern Turkey. Actually, it's a sleeping volcano, which means it isn't erupting right now. It is 16,845 feet high and has two peaks known fondly as Great Ararat and Little Ararat. Both peaks are covered with snow all year long.

Quest for the Lost Ark

Many people have studied Mount Ararat in the hopes of finding some part of the ark still there. Some researchers and explorers think that parts of the ark are frozen in an ice field near a spot on the mountain called Ahora Gorge. Explorers have climbed the mountain up past 10,000 feet to the snowy peaks. In 1980 former NASA astronaut James Irwin led an expedition up the mountain to find the ark.

Many climbers, who have been to Ararat during hot summers when the glacier ice slowly melts down, have claimed to have seen large wood planks. Some have even said they have walked on the roof of the ice-trapped ark. Airplane pilots also have claimed they have glimpsed the ark from the air. But to date there still is no clear proof that it is there.

Replanting

God asked Noah to save the animals, but what about the plants? Talk about waterlogged! No doubt Noah had some seeds and plants on board for feeding the animals. Some seeds can float, and even soaked in saltwater they can still sprout. Some plants can even replant themselves by making new roots from other parts, like branches. Now that is a veggie tale!

EXP.
6 APR
2009
PERMITTED
ENTRY AS
VISITOR ONLY
MT. ARARAT

- Kauai, Hawaii averages 350 rainy days a year!

- One of the longest-lasting rainbows on record appeared for three hours! It was reported in northern Wales in 1974.

- Other ancient kingdoms and civilizations tell stories about a great flood as well.

DID YOU KNOW

ALONG CAME NIMROD!

God promised Noah he would never again destroy the whole earth with another flood, and he gave us a rainbow as a sign of that promise. After the flood, some of Noah's family traveled five hundred miles from Mount Ararat back down the Tigris River and settled close to where they had once lived in a place now called the Fertile Crescent. They took up the family biz of farming again.

Table of Nations

Noah's three sons, Japheth, Ham, Shem, and their offspring were the start of some pretty important ancient nations. Japheth would be the father of the people that settled in the north—Europe and parts of Asia. Ham's offspring would later be found along the eastern shores of the Mediterranean and further into Arabia, Egypt, and Africa. Noah's eldest son Shem would be the father of the Jews, Assyrians, Syrians, and Elamites along the Euphrates Valley. That's what you call a hometown boy. Things were going well for the Noah family for many generations until a relative named Nimrod came along.

Rumor has it that Nimrod was a pretty important guy—really tough and extremely

Table of Nations and the Cities that Nimrod Built

JAPETH

BLACK SEA

CASPIAN SEA

Mt. Ararat

Nineveh
Resen
Rehoboth Ir
Calah

FERTILE CRESCENT

MEDITERRANEAN SEA

Tigris River

Babylon
Akkad
Calneh
Erech

Euphrates River

SHEM

HAM

RED SEA

| 0 | 100 | 200 | 300 | 400 miles |

| 0 | 200 | 400 | 600 kilometers |

busy. He built not just one city, but all kinds of cities—Babylon, Erech, Akkad, and Calneh in Shinar, and then on to Assyria where he built Rehoboth Ir, Calah, Resen, and Nineveh. Wow! Didn't this guy ever take a coffee break? (Caught ya! They didn't have coffee back then!)

That's not to say Nimrod had an ego but … he made himself the big bad ruler over everything, which he called "the Land of Nimrod." Everybody in Nimrod was speaking the same language and working hard.

Many Bible scholars believe it was Nimrod who built a tower so tall it would reach heaven. The idea being that with a tower like that, you could almost be God. Quick! Somebody sound the mega-ego alarm! This tower was trouble with a capital "T." God saw how vain and self-important these people had become. What was God going to do about this?

Scattered!

Okay, okay, God didn't let the tower fall down on top of anybody. This isn't the movies! But as punishment for their pride, God stopped the people from finishing the tower by suddenly giving different groups different languages to speak. Nobody could understand what the other group was saying! Confused and completely misunderstood, the people left the area and traveled far away, all mumbling in different languages as they went. That's how the world got separated into so many different languages.

Today more than six thousand languages are spoken around the world. We told you that tower was trouble! Different languages, ways of doing things, and far-off lands now separated people. Could the human race ever be reunited again as one people under God? Did God have a plan? Of course!

joke

What message is the same from left to right, right to left, upside down, and right-side up?

SOS

Talk About Towering Towers!

Hey, is there anything left of the Tower of Babel? Many archaeologists have searched the ancient cities of Nimrod to find the ruins of the tower. They have found thirty younger towers called ziggurats (meaning "mountain peak"). They are basically towers built out of mountains of brick. Some are more than four thousand years old, and one tower was seventy feet tall. That was impressive for back then! But none of the towers found were old enough to be the Tower of Babel.

BABYLO

IMMIGRATION

11 05 200

PERMITTED EN
AS VISITOR O

- The Tower of Babel is the Hebrew name for Babylon. Today we relate the word "babble" to talking nonsense.

- One of the greatest linguists (someone who speaks many languages) was Dr. Harold Williams of New Zealand, who spoke fifty-eight languages.

CANAAN OR BUST

God had a plan for the now-scattered people of the Earth, but to get that plan started, he had to choose one nation that he could teach and build a close and loving relationship with. That relationship started with one good man called Abram. He lived in a not-so-small city called Ur along the lower part of the Euphrates River. Abram lived between fifteen hundred to two thousand years before Jesus lived … or said another way, 1500 to 2000 B.C. (before Christ). (The years after Christ lived are called A.D., for the Latin phrase anno Domini, meaning "in the year of the Lord.")

joke

What did Abraham say when he wanted to get his sheep's attention?

"Hey, ewe!"

Abram's father decided to pack up the entire family, including Abram and his wife Sarai, and travel up the Tigris or Euphrates River to a city called Haran. Before you picture the entire family wearing out their sandals hiking three hundred miles, they did have donkeys and camels for carrying goods and riding on. Abram stayed only fifteen years until his father died.

Then God told Abram to trust and follow his directions exactly. Abram, his wife, and his nephew Lot were soon on the

Two possible routes from Ur to Haran

0   100   200 miles
0   100   200 kilometers

▲ Mt. Ararat

Haran

Nineveh

CYPRUS

Euphrates River

Tigris River

Asshur

THE GREAT SEA (MEDITERRANEAN SEA)

Damascus

Hazor

CANAAN

Babylon

Ramoth-Gilead
Succoth
Shechem

Nippur

Route to Egypt

Ur

EGYPT   ARABIAN DESERT

Nile R.

Abraham's Journey

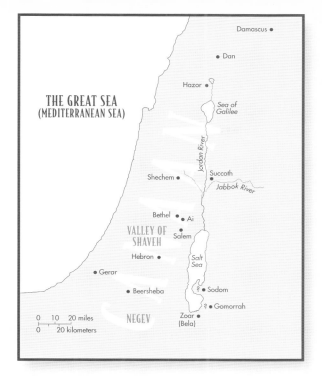

The Great Sea (Mediterranean Sea) map showing: Damascus, Dan, Hazor, Sea of Galilee, Jordan River, Shechem, Succoth, Jabbok River, Bethel, Ai, Valley of Shaveh, Salem, Hebron, Salt Sea, Gerar, Beersheba, Sodom, Gomorrah, Zoar (Bela), Negev

move to a new land God promised to give them. They lived in tents and traveled with their herd of sheep. Finally, about four hundred miles later, they reached a place called Canaan along the Mediterranean Sea, which is now where the countries of Israel, Lebanon, and Syria meet the sea. It would have been a great place except for one small problem. There was a famine—no food to be found anywhere!

So Abram trekked on south almost three hundred miles and found good grazing land plus a few adventures (some of the not-so-nice kind) in the land of Egypt. Egypt then is just where you find the country of Egypt today.

During their Egyptian tour, their herds increased, so Abram and Lot were now wealthy men. Get a big tent, because between family members and servants, we're talking about a thousand people camping together. Not to mention all those sheep! So Abram's clan went back to Canaan while Lot's clan went to a place called Jordan a little further inland. They split the sheep.

Now Canaan was a busy place. The many tribes that lived there constantly fought over land and water. But God promised Abram that he would

be the father of an entire nation of people and that Canaan would be his alone. But Abram had to stay true to God and worship him only (no sneaking in foreign idols). Abram agreed to everything God asked. God changed Abram's name to Abraham, which means "father of many."

God gave the very old Abraham and his wife a son named Isaac, and that was the start of many big things, just as God had promised.

Sodom and Gomorrah

Sodom and Gomorrah were two cities that might have been near the southern end of the Dead Sea in what is now part of the country of Israel.

The citizens of Sodom and Gomorrah were incredibly wicked. It seems the stories of the Flood made no impression on them. So God decided to completely destroy the two cities. The cities were hit by a storm of burning sulfur.

Near the Dead Sea archaeologists have found city ruins that are covered in a black, charcoal substance. Are they the remains of those two destroyed cities? Researchers are working hard to find out.

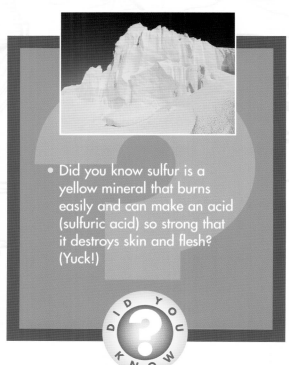

- Did you know sulfur is a yellow mineral that burns easily and can make an acid (sulfuric acid) so strong that it destroys skin and flesh? (Yuck!)

DID YOU KNOW

Abraham's son Isaac grew up and had two boys of his own, Jacob and Esau. Then Jacob grew up and had lots of boys—twelve, in fact. These boys would be the start of the twelve tribes of Israel. But one special son was going to have an adventure of a lifetime.

Handsome and smart, seventeen-year-old Joseph was sold by his eleven very jealous brothers to some Ishmaelite slave traders who often traveled to Egypt's capital city of Raamses.

Egyptian Power

Egypt was a desert kingdom built along a 750-mile stretch of the Nile River. Life along the Nile centered around a ten-mile-wide strip of rich farmland on either side of the river. Egypt had been one of the great powers of the ancient world for hundreds and hundreds of years before Joseph was dragged there.

Egyptians built great cities for the living and even greater tombs and temples for their dead. Their armies conquered many of the neighboring kingdoms and lands. Egyptian merchants sailed across the Mediterranean Sea, trading the gold, silver, ivory, copper, spices, precious stones, expensive woods, and exotic animals they took from Africa. Egypt = wealth and power.

Egypt in Ruins

Ancient visitors to Egypt like Joseph were impressed with the famous pyramids and Sphinx, which were already more than a thousand years old. Even the sixty-six-foot-tall Sphinx was mostly buried in desert sands. The largest pyramid, belonging to a pharaoh named Khufu, was more than 450 feet tall. It may have taken a crew of a hundred thousand slaves to position all the fifteen-ton blocks of stone that created the mountain-sized tomb. But don't forget there are also more than a dozen other amazing ruins along the Nile. Awesome work!

The Stuff Dreams Are Made Of

Joseph worked hard at everything he did, and with God's help, he understood the meaning of some odd dreams the pharaoh was having. Egypt was heading for a big-time famine! Pharaoh made Joseph the manager of the entire country. During the famine, Joseph forgave his brothers and brought the entire family back to Egypt to share his success. Joseph understood that his early hardships were all part of God's plan for him. Now with God's help, he could help his family. What a plan!

THE PYRAMIDS

The Sphinx

DID YOU KNOW?

joke

Where do mummies go swimming?

In the
Dead Sea.

EGYPT
06 JUL 2011

THE GREAT SEA
(MEDITERRANEAN SEA)

CANAAN

Giza

Memphis

EGYPT

El-Amarna
(Akhetaton)

Nile River

Luxor

RED SEA

Ruins in Egypt

Search For The Mummy

Joseph lived to be 110 years old. When he died, he was embalmed Egyptian style. In other words, Joseph became what we call today a mummy. After a person died, Egyptians had a precise way of removing the organs, drying out the body, and wrapping the body with special spices, oils, and cloth. This stopped the body from decaying away. If you were an important person, you were placed in a fancy tomb. Have they found Joseph's tomb in Egypt?

Archaeologists have found a small pyramid tomb set in what would have been the garden of a palace. A statue found in the tomb is of a man dressed in the style of the colorful clothes of Joseph's people—not the plain white of the Egyptians. There was no mummy found because when Joseph's people left Egypt more than four hundred years later, they took his body with them. Could this really be Joseph's tomb?

EXIT (EXODUS) OUT OF EGYPT

Joseph brought his people to Egypt. Now a man named Moses was about to help the Israelites leave Egypt. It had been four hundred years since Joseph, and sadly, his good work had long been forgotten. Now the new pharaohs had made the Hebrews slaves and worked them hard making bricks. But with God's help, Moses pressured Pharoah into letting the Israelites leave Egypt. They were heading back to Canaan.

Let's stop and check out one of the most unusual sea battles in history. It was a dangerous journey for the Israelites escaping through Egypt. They stayed clear of trade routes and towns. You might say they went "off road" through the wilds of the Sinai Desert. But God was ahead of them, guiding them by day with a towering pillar of cloud by day and with a pillar of fire by night. God told them to camp between the Red Sea and a place called Migdol. Why there? It was less than a hundred miles from where they started!

Pharaoh changed his mind and was in hot pursuit ready to wipe Moses off the map, so to speak. He couldn't believe his eyes when he saw the Israelites trapped against the sea with no way to escape. How stupid of them!

The Israelites were terrified, but Moses went into action and followed God's directions.

THE GREAT SEA (MEDITERRANEAN SEA)

CANAAN

Jordan River

Rabbah

Heshbon

Jericho

Mt. Nebo

Salt Sea

Beersheba

DESERT OF ZIN

GOSHEN

Zoan

Migdol

Rameses

Succoth

Pithom

Great Bitter Lake

Kadesh

Punon

Pyramids at Giza

On

Memphis

EGYPT

SINAI

Ezion Geber

Nile River

Marah

WILDERNESS OF SIN

Elim

Rephidim

Red Sea

Red Sea

-------- Route of the Exodus

0   20   40 miles

0   20   40 kilometers

Mt. Sinai (Horeb)

The Exodus Out of Egypt

He held his staff out over the sea and the waters parted, leaving a path of dry land to cross.

Many researchers feel the Gulf of Suez (part of the Red Sea) may have connected with the Bitter Lakes, and somewhere near the lakes is where Moses crossed the Red Sea.

When everyone was safely across, God allowed Pharaoh and his troops to enter the water. God made chariot wheels fall off and made tough war horses too frightened to control. It was a mess! Pharaoh suddenly realized he was fighting this battle with God! The water flowed back and swept the Egyptian army into the sea.

Dinner Included

The Israelites continued their journey into the Sinai Desert. One problem! There isn't a whole lot for a million people to eat in the desert. So after they spent a month of traveling and eating all their food, God gave them a miracle called manna. It fell with the dew each night and was gathered in the morning. Manna was small round flakes that tasted like honey and wafers. Manna recipes anyone? The word manna came from the Israelite phrase "man-hu?" meaning, "What is it?" We still don't know.

The Mountain

Moses led his people back to the pastureland of his wife's people in Midian near the base of Mount Sinai. Today Midian is found along the coast of Jordan and Saudi Arabia. More than a dozen mountains have been suggested as the mountain that Moses climbed to receive the Ten Commandments or Laws from God.

joke

How do you cut the ocean in two?

With a sea-saw.

down their jewelry. Not a good idea! But that was only the start of many problems. The last straw was when some of Moses' spies came back from Canaan and convinced the people not to go there. Here they were at Kadesh on the edge of God's Promised Land and nobody wanted to go. God became angry at their constant unbelief and distrust. He made the Israelites wander in the wilderness between Mount Sinai and the Jordan River for forty years before he allowed them to cross the river into Canaan.

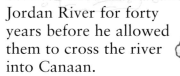

- The desert rocks heated by the sun have been known to reach temperatures as high as 180° F.

- The camel is often called the ship of the desert. With a single rider, it can travel a hundred miles a day. As a pack animal, it can carry loads up to a thousand pounds.

DID YOU KNOW

Mount Sinai

Jordan River

While Moses was up on the mountain, the restless Israelites made a golden calf idol by melting

God wanted Moses and his people to have a place to worship him even when they were on the move. So God instructed Moses to build a special holy chest called the Ark of the Covenant. It was beautiful and made with carved wood overlaid with gold. It was God's throne on earth where the Israelites could go and pray. Inside this box was the Ten Commandments, a pot of manna, and Aaron's staff, which had budded. God also ordered an amazing tent to be built as a mobile temple.

Next stop … the Promised Land. Moses never entered the Promised Land, but he left a strong leader by the name of Joshua in charge. Joshua had been born an Egyptian slave, but now he was a man of God and a brilliant leader in battle. Joshua took his people across the Jordan River to God's Promised Land. One small problem—there were already people living there. Joshua got busy getting back Canaan for his people.

joke

Why was the king of Jericho upset?

His career was in ruins.

Battle at Jericho

Joshua's first big battle in 1406 B.C. was a smashing success! Joshua and his men surrounded the Canaanite city of Jericho. The idea of surrounding or "taking siege" of a city was to stop food and other supplies from getting inside. Basically, the idea was to hang out long enough and maybe the people inside would eventually surrender. A siege can take months, depending on how much food and water the city has inside. But God had another plan.

THE GREAT SEA (MEDITERRANEAN SEA)

0 25 50 75 mi.
0 25 50 75 100 km.

Kedesh
Hazor
Merom
BASHAN
Sea of Kinnereth
Mt. Tabor
Edrei
Mt. Gilboa
Jordan R.
Shechem
Shiloh
Bethel
Gibeon
Ai
Gilgal?
Abel Shittim
Beth Horon
Jericho
Heshbon
AMMON
Jarmuth
Jerusalem
Mt. Nebo
Azekah
Libnah?
Jahaz?
Lachish
Hebron
PHILISTIA
Eglon?
Makkedah?
Dibon
Besor Br.
Debir?
Arnon R.
Beersheba
Salt Sea
MOAB
Iye Abarim?
DESERT OF ZIN
Zered Br.
EDOM
DESERT OF SHUR
Oboth?
Punon
Kadesh Barnea
DESERT OF PARAN
SINAI
Ezion Geber

Area controlled by ancient Israel
→ Entry into and conquest of Canaan
✕ Battle

Joshua's Conquest of Canaan

In ancient times Jericho was a beautiful walled city in a grove of palm trees. God told Joshua to march around the city with his men for six days.

On the seventh day a strange sight greeted the people in the city. They watched as Joshua's tough soldiers marched around their city seven times. They were shouting and priests were blowing horn trumpets while they carried a strange golden box (the ark). This wasn't like any siege they'd had before. What was up with these Israelites?

Apparently, the Israelites had the right stuff, because the walls of the city came crashing down, and Joshua and his men took the city. God had won yet another battle for his people.

There were many battles fought during the ten to fifteen years it took Joshua to win Canaan. He conquered six nations and thirty-one kings. They fought the Canaanites, Moabites, Ammonites, and Philistines. Joshua didn't win every battle or all of Canaan, for that matter. But for now, he divided his new land between eleven of the twelve tribes of Israel.

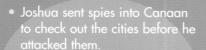

Jericho

The priestly tribe of Levi received no land. The different tribes went off and built villages and cities of their own. They began to farm the land God had given them. But could the Israelites stay true to God and his Law, or would they try the new and strange ways of some of their neighbors? Could they resist temptation?

EXP. 20 APR 2002

PERMITTED ENTRY AS VISITOR ONLY

JERICHO

- Joshua sent spies into Canaan to check out the cities before he attacked them.

- Current-day Jericho is one of the lowest cities in the world at eight hundred feet below the level of the ocean.

DID YOU KNOW

After Joshua died, the twelve tribes just couldn't seem to get their act together. Some began to worship the gods of their neighbors, and still others fought among themselves. It was another big mess. So God appointed good men to rule or judge over each area. They would tend to matters concerning that tribe and their neighbors. The tribes managed to stick together for three hundred years during this time of the judges, but eventually, they wanted a king to rule over all the tribes.

Enter God's faithful holy man—the prophet Samuel. He was led by God to meet a man named Saul from the tribe of Benjamin. Israel's first king was tall, handsome, and from an important family. Saul was a good king for a while, but something happened. Saul became vain and self-important. He turned into a bad king.

God decided a new king must be found and sent Samuel on a secret mission to find him. Samuel found their new king in a small village called Bethlehem. David was only a shepherd boy at the time, but Samuel knew God wanted this young man to become the future king. So Samuel secretly anointed David as king.

David's Day

David was still a teenager when his older brothers were called to another war with the Philistines. Not again! The Philistines lived along the ocean coast and were a tough group. This time both sides faced off on the rolling hills on either side of a wide valley called Elah. The Philistines sent a giant of a man named Goliath down into the valley to tease and challenge one Israelite to fight him to decide the battle. Goliath was 9 feet tall,

joke

What did the helmet say to the soldier when they went into battle?

You're putting me on!

his helmet and armor weighed 125 pounds, and his spear was an amazing 15 pounds!

While David was visiting his older brothers, he became angry that this Philistine bully was making fun of the army of God. David volunteered to fight. Out he went, and with one whoosh of his sling, he sent a stone into Goliath's forehead, killing the giant. It was a short but impressive fight. David was an instant hero! It was a long, hard road avoiding a jealous King Saul, but finally David became king. He was thirty years old when he took the throne, and he ruled Israel for forty years.

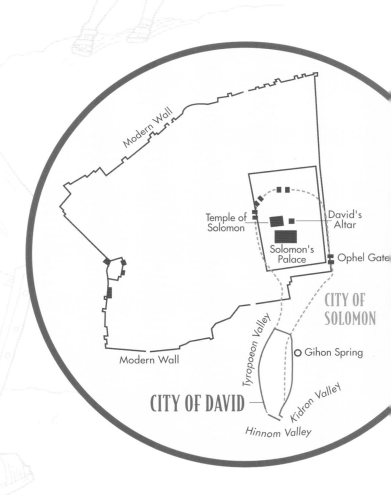

Kingdom of David and Solomon

THE GREAT SEA
(MEDITERRANEAN SEA)

HAMATH

Saul's kingdom

David and Solomon's kingdom

Territory under Solomon's control

0   20   40   60   80 mi.
0 20 40 60 80 100 km.

all of present-day Israel, Lebanon, and the lower part of Syria. He made Israel the most powerful kingdom on earth!

Jerusalem

What would you do if you found a city on the highest plateau in all the land with steep ravines on both sides and secret tunnels that brought water into the city during times of war? You'd do what David did. You'd make it a fortress city that nobody could attack! This spot had already been a village or city for thousands of years before David took over. The Egyptians record the city as being called Urusalim. David took the Jebusite city, which was then called Jerusalem. After his victory, many people called it the city of David. Jerusalem has been located in the same spot for almost seven thousand years. David brought the Ark of the Covenant to stay in his safe new city.

David fought battles with every kingdom that went against Israel and won! If David were king today, he would have ruled over

JERUSALEM
[31 OCT 1996]
IMMIGRATION OFFICER

Jerusalem

Let's put on the brakes at the year 1000 B.C. At that time in Israel, one of their most successful kings ruled with wisdom and power. David's son Solomon was a great ruler! When God asked Solomon what he wanted in the entire world, Solomon asked for wisdom to help him rule his people. He got it! People came from neighboring kingdoms just to hear him speak because he was so wise. His ships controlled the oceans along the coasts of Arabia, India, and Africa. He had gold mines in Saudi Arabia that made him extremely wealthy. Solomon built a beautiful temple to house the Ark of the Covenant. He pleased God with almost everything he did. So life was good for Israel under Solomon's rule.

joke

Where were Solomon's temples?

On his head.

Africa

The Nubians in the land of Cush in Africa were about to break free of Egyptian rule to make a new and powerful kingdom of their own. They even built their own large pyramids and were trading gold and ivory to far-off lands.

India

India was a busy place. About one-fourth of the entire world's population lived in India! In fact, many different foreign tribes of people moved into India and took over, much like the Israelites did in Canaan. But this change in people and rulers helped make India a nation of excellent farmers, boat builders, and metal workers.

China

Things were happening in China along the Hwang-Ho (Big Yellow River). The country was broken up into a hundred clans or big, related families. Wealthy families owned land and impressive houses. Often there were little wars between the clans over land and power. China at that time was known for its beautiful art and writings.

Mediterranean Sea

Along what was then known as the Great Sea was a group of cities joined together to make a nation called Phoenicia. What did they do? They were the sailors of the ancient world! Their galley ships used a combination of sails and oars to power them around so they could trade with just about everybody. They went to Italy, Greece, Africa, and as far away as the Atlantic Ocean along the coast of Spain. Some think they even explored the ocean clear up to Great Britain.

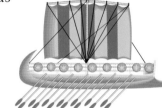

Americas

What was happening in North, Central, and South America at that time? Many of the people in North America were still living a life of hunting and gathering food in small communities. Some were building farming villages and towns.

But really big things were happening in the jungles of Mexico. A big kingdom was forming called the Olmecs. They built huge temples and cities. Their stonework was beautiful and mysterious. We know they wrote in a form of hieroglyphics (ancient writing), but no one has been able to translate it.

Even though God was building a close relationship with Israel, he loved all the people of the world. God was using Israel to help bring everybody back to him free of sin. It was all part of the plan.

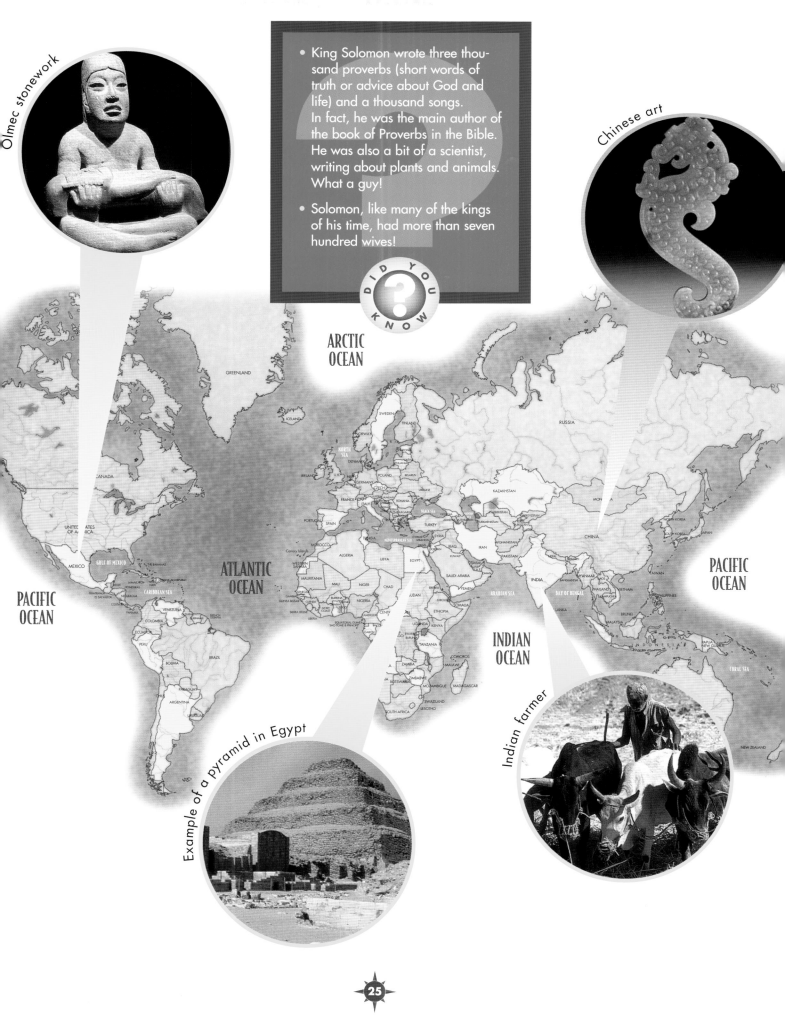

Olmec stonework

Chinese art

ARCTIC OCEAN

GREENLAND

ICELAND

SWEDEN
FINLAND
NORWAY
RUSSIA

NORTH SEA
DENMARK
IRELAND
U.K.
POLAND
BELARUS

CANADA

FRANCE
CZECH
UKRAINE
KAZAKHSTAN
MONGOLIA

PORTUGAL
SPAIN
ITALY
ROMANIA
TURKEY

UNITED STATES OF AMERICA

MOROCCO
MEDITERRANEAN SEA
SYRIA
IRAQ
IRAN
AFGHANISTAN
CHINA
NORTH KOREA
SOUTH KOREA
JAPAN

MEXICO
GULF OF MEXICO
THE BAHAMAS
ALGERIA
LIBYA
EGYPT
SAUDI ARABIA
PAKISTAN

Canary Islands
WESTERN SAHARA
MAURITANIA
MALI
NIGER
CHAD
SUDAN
YEMEN
OMAN
INDIA
MYANMAR
TAIWAN

CARIBBEAN SEA
BELIZE
JAMAICA
HAITI
SENEGAL
BURKINA
NIGERIA
ARABIAN SEA
BAY OF BENGAL
THAILAND
VIETNAM
PHILIPPINES

GUATEMALA
HONDURAS
EL SALVADOR
NICARAGUA
COSTA RICA
PANAMA
GUINEA-BISSAU
IVORY COAST
SIERRA LEONE
CAMEROON
CENTRAL
ETHIOPIA
SOMALIA
SRI LANKA
BRUNEI
MALAYSIA

VENEZUELA
FRENCH GUIANA
GABON
EQUATORIAL GUINEA
SAO TOME & PRINCIPE
UGANDA
KENYA
INDONESIA
PAPUA NEW GUINEA

COLOMBIA
ECUADOR
PERU
RWANDA
BURUNDI
TANZANIA

ATLANTIC OCEAN

BRAZIL
BOLIVIA
ZAMBIA
COMOROS
MALAWI
CORAL SEA

PARAGUAY
ZIMBABWE
MOZAMBIQUE
MADAGASCAR

CHILE
BOTSWANA
SWAZILAND

ARGENTINA
SOUTH AFRICA
LESOTHO

URUGUAY

NEW ZEALAND

PACIFIC OCEAN

PACIFIC OCEAN

INDIAN OCEAN

Example of a pyramid in Egypt

Indian farmer

GETTING ALONG?

If things were very good when Solomon was king, they went really bad after he died. Solomon's son Rehoboam had barely got the old seat warm on the throne when trouble hit. Although in many, many ways, Solomon was a good king, some of the tribes found him stern and heavy-handed with his taxes. Solomon had also made the mistake of not following God's will in every aspect of his life. God promised Solomon that his kingdom would be divided after his death. And it was!

Ten of the twelve tribes decided that they wanted to go it alone and start their own kingdom. Perhaps Solomon's ex-chief superintendent by the name of Jeroboam had something to do with that. He had plotted to become king himself, but when his plots were discovered, he fled to Egypt. Now the ten tribes invited him back to be the king of the new kingdom of Israel.

Meanwhile from Jerusalem, Solomon's son Rehoboam ruled two faithful tribes. This smaller kingdom was called Judah.

Kingdom of Judah

The kingdom of Judah was mouse-sized, with only about three hundred square miles, compared to the thirteen-thousand-square-mile empire that Solomon had built. Rehoboam ruled for only seventeen troubled-filled years. To protect his little piece of kingdom, he built guarded fortresses in sight of each other to keep invaders out. Did it work? More on that later.

Kingdom of Israel

Sneaky Jeroboam was invited back from his time-out in Egypt to be made king of Israel.

The Kingdoms of Israel and Judah

He ruled more land and people than poor Rehoboam. The kingdom of Israel was about 9,375 square miles. Jeroboam made the city of Shechem his capital because it was in a protected mountain valley.

He encouraged his people to worship the golden calves he built so his people would stop going to Solomon's temple in Jerusalem to worship God. That was really getting off on the wrong foot. This king was leading God's people in the completely wrong direction. He was bad news!

Ark of the Covenant
representation in stone

Where Is the Ark Today?

For some mysterious reason, the Ark of the Covenant drops out of history after Solomon's time. What happened to it? Where did it go? And most importantly, who took it out of Solomon's temple? Researchers have many ideas.

King Jeroboam encouraged his friend Shishak I, pharaoh of Egypt, to go attack Judah. Hey, what are good neighbors for? Shishak did attack Judah and raided Jerusalem. He took treasures from the royal palace and Solomon's temple. Some think he may have taken the ark as well.

Others think that maybe for safety, the ark was hidden in a secret stone tunnel deep underneath Jerusalem. That's some secret! Nobody has found it!

Still others think that when the Queen of Sheba (Ethiopia) visited King Solomon, a relationship was formed between the two kingdoms and the ark was sent to Africa for safekeeping.

There are many ideas as to what happened to the ark, but nobody has ever found it. It may be a mystery that is never solved.

joke

What kind of party did Judah want to give Pharoah Shishak?

A going-away party!

- When Pharaoh Shishak attacked Judah, he destroyed 150 towns and villages. He may have walked away with two hundred tons of Solomon's gold and silver.

- Because gold has been constantly remelted and made into new objects over thousands of years, some of the gold in your jewelry today may be part of Solomon's gold.

DID YOU KNOW

Kings may win or inherit kingdoms, but God makes prophets. Who are prophets? Good and holy men whom God picks to tell kings and people what's on his heart. For almost every bad king, there was one of God's prophets telling him what God really wanted.

The kingdom of Israel started out worshipping the Canaanite storm god Baal, and that wickedness was passed down from one king to another. So God sent the prophet Elijah to warn King Ahab to get right with God or else. Ahab didn't listen, so God sent a three and a half-year drought (a long time with no rain). It was very hard on the people. But no matter what God did to get Ahab's attention, Ahab and his son still did wrong things.

The kingdom of Israel lasted for two hundred years, and in all that time, not one of its nineteen kings worshiped God. And it wasn't like God didn't send many more prophets like Elisha, Hosea, Isaiah, and Micah to help them get right. What could God do with such disobedient and headstrong people?

Watch Out for the Assyrians

Let's pay a visit to the new guys on the Canaanite street. In a steep mountain area, a group of farmers called themselves the Assyrians. They were very protective of their land. But soon protecting their own territory turned into raiding their neighbors. And then just

taking things wasn't enough for them. The Assyrians became a fighting machine that took over other people's land. They grew into an empire that showed no mercy to their neighbors for three hundred years.

A divided kingdom like Judah and Israel was an easy target for the Assyrians. The cities of Israel were attacked and destroyed, and the people were taken away as slaves. The Assyrian king sent his own people to live in Israel. So the kingdom of Israel was completely gone. But it was all part of what God said would happen to Israel if they didn't follow his ways.

Kingdom of Judah

What about the smaller kingdom of Judah? Solomon's grandson Abijah and great-grandson Jehoshaphat were good kings who followed God's ways, and that's why God blessed their kingdom.

But later, a king named Jehoram married an evil princess from Israel who brought her

- The prophet Elijah was taken up to heaven by a whirlwind.

- One of the largest nuggets of gold ever found weighed 220 pounds.

- In the sixties an area called Sahel in Africa had the longest drought in 150 years, lasting twelve years.

DID YOU KNOW?

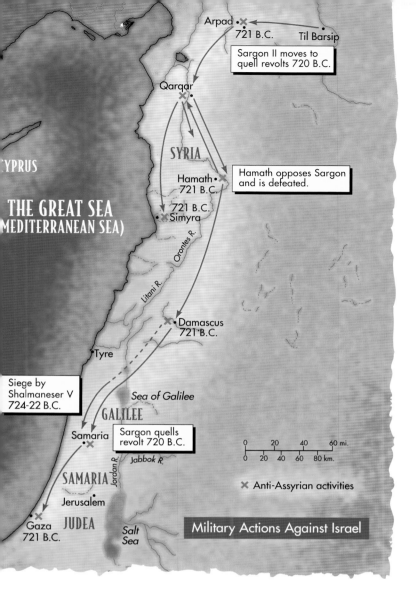

Arpad
721 B.C. • ✕ ← • Til Barsip

Sargon II moves to
quell revolts 720 B.C.

Qarqar
✕

SYRIA

Hamath opposes Sargon
and is defeated.

Hamath •
721 B.C.

721 B.C.
✕ Simyra

CYPRUS

THE GREAT SEA
(MEDITERRANEAN SEA)

Orontes R.

Litani R.

• **Damascus**
721 B.C.

• Tyre

Siege by
Shalmaneser V
724-22 B.C.

Sea of Galilee

GALILEE

• Samaria
✕

Sargon quells
revolt 720 B.C.

Jabbok R.

Jordan R.

SAMARIA

• Jerusalem

✕
Gaza **JUDEA** *Salt*
721 B.C. *Sea*

0   20   40   60 mi.
0 20 40 60 80 km.

✕ Anti-Assyrian activities

Military Actions Against Israel

But it doesn't pay to pay off bullies, because two years later the king of Assyria was back for more. But this time Hezekiah was smart and prayed instead of paid. God heard his prayers and that night killed 185,000 Assyrian soldiers. The frightened king of Assyria ran back home with a much smaller army. But the kingdom of Judah would soon face an even bigger bully named Babylon!

How many kings can you put in an empty cage?

One. After that the cage isn't empty anymore.

---

wicked ways. Then came a series of really, really bad kings and queens. One queen even tried to kill all her grandchildren! The kingdom of Judah flip-flopped from good kings to bad kings.

To keep Assyria happy and out of their country, the kings of Judah paid them in gold and silver. But one good king named Hezekiah refused to pay. The Assyrians got just a "little" upset and attacked forty-six cities in Judah. They captured Hezekiah and kept him in a large birdcage! He finally paid the Assyrians eleven tons of silver and a ton of gold just to make them leave his kingdom.

ENTRY
PERMITTED
AS VISITOR
JUDAH
23 09 1997

Before you start thinking the kingdom of Judah had it easy compared to Israel, think again. Let's pop in and see what was happening around 586 B.C. The big bad Assyrians had made a huge mistake by ignoring the growing power of a smaller kingdom called Babylon. The Babylonians were getting more powerful every day, and in one huge move, they took over Assyria, Judah, and Egypt.

Babylonian Bio

The Babylonians controlled a large triangular section of land between the Persian Gulf, along the Red Sea, and the inland coast of the Mediterranean Sea. The king of Babylon had a huge army always ready for his every command. The capital of Babylon built near the Euphrates River was one of the most impressive cities of its day. It covered 2,100 acres of land, and as many as 200,000 people may have lived there. It had paved roads and even sidewalks. A brick wall twenty-one feet thick and fifty-nine feet tall protected the inner city. The city even had a moat, which was 150 feet wide. This was a city fit for a powerful ruler.

Nebuchadnezzar

The king of Judah tried to make a stand and refused to give Babylon any payment to honor their power. This really upset the Babylonian king Nebuchadnezzar! He wanted payment, he wanted respect, and he wanted it now! So he attacked Jerusalem, destroyed Solomon's beautiful temple, and killed Judah's King Jehoiakim. The prophets had warned Judah that they had to stay right with God. But once again Judah ignored God's prophets.

Nebuchadnezzar wasn't going to stand for any more trouble from Judah. After attacking

joke

Why is it so wet in the kingdoms of Judah and Israel?

Because of all the kings and queens who reigned there.

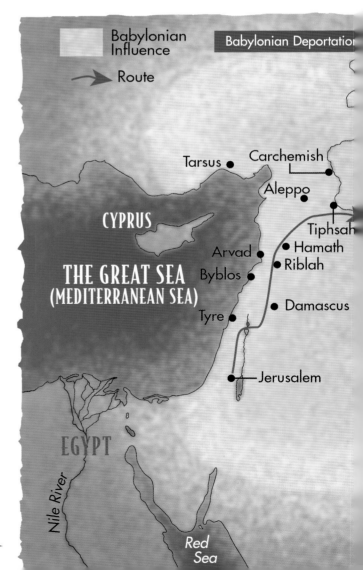

Jerusalem, he captured ten thousand of Judah's princes, officers, and important families. They were taken to his capital city of Babylon. So like Israel, the kingdom of Judah was no more. But don't worry! God sent with his people a wise prophet named Ezekiel to help them.

Nebuchadnezzar wanted the young men of Judah to be trained as Babylonians in all things. Four brave guys named Daniel, Hananiah, Mishael, and Azariah found ways to stay faithful to the Law of God even while they lived in Babylon. Because of this, God gave them success and honor. Daniel even became King Nebuchadnezzar's friend and close adviser.

Sadly, the great kingdom that David and his son Solomon had built lasted only four hundred years before being destroyed—all because the kings and people of Israel and Judah wouldn't stay true to God's will.

- One of the seven wonders of the ancient world was the Babylonian hanging gardens that were planted on five stacked terraces. Each terrace was fifty feet tall. It looked like a mountain of plants and trees. Today we have only ruins to tell of the beauty of Babylon.

- It took Nebuchadnezzar thirteen years of siege to take the seaside city of Tyre.

DID YOU KNOW?

The people of Judah were forced to stay in Babylon for seventy years. Then a new growing empire called Persia attacked the Babylonians. The Persian king Cyrus let God's people go. Way to go, Cyrus! But had they learned their lesson that each person—king or commoner—must make a personal choice to have a good and faithful relationship with God?

Meeting Place

When Solomon's temple was destroyed and the people of Israel and Judah were scattered to different kingdoms, God's faithful still wanted to worship together and keep their faith alive. But they had no tabernacle, temple, or homeland. In Babylon they built synagogues as holy meeting places. These meeting places kept the people's faith alive and kept them close to God when far from home.

▲ Mt. Ararat

zan

Nineveh

Tigris River

Asshur

Arrapkha

Ecbatana

Behistun

Babylon

BABYLONIA

Nippur

Erech

Ur

N DESERT

Lower Sea

0   100   200 miles

0   100   200 kilometers

PACK YOUR BAGS! WE'RE GOING HOME!

God's people were finally going home and taking back with them some of the things Nebuchadnezzar had stolen from the temple in Jerusalem. The king of Persia even gave them money to rebuild their city. About five thousand people returned to Jerusalem to start a new life. They rebuilt the city wall and, most importantly, the temple. Did everybody return home? Some people decided to remain in Babylon and make small communities of their own.

This was an exciting time for the new and improved kingdom of Judah because they had rulers who worshiped God and knew how to run a good kingdom. It was a fresh beginning, and they were making things right with God.

But don't get too comfortable! There was yet another new empire heading their way and getting ready to take over around the year 336 B.C. An amazing Greek soldier and leader named Alexander the Great was about to change the world. From his homeland in Greece, Alexander traveled with 35,000 soldiers (not exactly traveling light) around the Mediterranean Sea to attack and control kingdom after kingdom. That included Persia, Egypt, and, you guessed it, Judah. Alexander soon had the ancient world in his hands. He wanted to bring the Greek way of life to the world. And he did just that. Soon everybody was speaking, writing, and doing things just like the Greeks! Alexander died when he was only thirty-three years old.

His generals split up his empire, and little Judah was first ruled by one group and then another. Their new temple was soon filled with Greek idols.

joke

Is it true that Alexander the Great wouldn't hurt an army if they ran away from him?

Sure, if they ran fast enough!

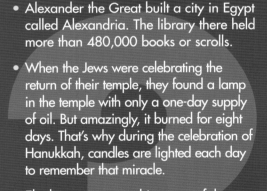

- Alexander the Great built a city in Egypt called Alexandria. The library there held more than 480,000 books or scrolls.

- When the Jews were celebrating the return of their temple, they found a lamp in the temple with only a one-day supply of oil. But amazingly, it burned for eight days. That's why during the celebration of Hanukkah, candles are lighted each day to remember that miracle.

- Elephants were used in some of the battles against Judas Maccabeus.

DID YOU KNOW ?

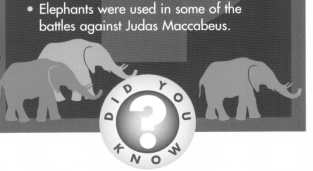

Alexandria

THRACE

BLACK SEA

SCYTHIA

MACEDONIA

ella

GREECE

Athens

Sparta

CRETE

Troy 334 B.C.
PHYRGIA Gordium Ancyra
Pergamum
Sardis Tyana
Ephesus Miletus
Perge Aspendus Tarsus
Halicarnussus Side
Xanthus Phaselis
Issus 333 B.C. Thapsacus
SYRIA

CYPRUS
Sidon
332 B.C. Damascus COELE-SYRIA
Tyre PHOENICIA
Ptolemais Scythopolis
Dora
Caesarea
Azotus Sebaste
Ascalon Modin
Gaza Jerusalem
Marisa

THE GREAT SEA
(MEDITERRANEAN SEA)

Alexandria

Memphis

Siwa
Nile R.

EGYPT

ARMENIA

Gaugamela 331 B.C.
Arbola

Tigris R.

Cunaxa

Babylon
Euphrates R.
SUSIANA
BABYLONIA

Susa

ARABIAN DESERT

ARABIA

RED SEA

MEDIA
Ecbatana

Rhagae

HYRCANIA

Caspian Gates

PERSIA

Pasargadae

Persepolis
331 B.C.

Alexandria in Carmenia

GEDROSIA

Alexandria Rhambacia

Pattala

CASPIAN
SEA

ARAL
SEA

Oxus R.

Joxartes R.

329 B.C.
Alexandria Eschate

Maraca

Alexandria Margiana

PARTHIA

Alexandria Areion

328 B.C.
Bactra Alexandria Oxiana

BACTRIA

Ortospana
(Kabul)

ARACHOSIA
Alexandria Arachosion
330 B.C.

Alexandria Prophthasia

DRANGIANA

GHANDARA

Taxila
Bucephala 328 B.C.

Indus R.

Hydaspes R.

Hyphasis R.

INDIA

INDIAN OCEAN

Who Rules?

If we check back in around 167 B.C., we find something amazing! A priest named Mattathias was just plain fed up with being pushed around by every empire passing through. He and his five sons, Judas, Jonathan, Simon, John, and Eleazar, wanted to take back Jerusalem and free her from foreign rulers. You could call them the Freedom Family!

Mattathias got so angry that one day in his village he walked right up to a Greek altar and smashed it—right in front of the entire village. That started it! The fight was on, and it would take twenty-four years to win. Judas Maccabeus, one of Mattathias's sons, was brilliant on the battlefield. What a fighter!

What a leader! He just couldn't be beat! They won back Jerusalem, and the first thing they did was toss out all of the Greek stuff in God's temple. They made the temple clean of anything unholy and gave it back to God and his people. That victory celebration is now known as the Feast of Hanukkah. For the next hundred years, the grandsons and great-grandsons of Mattathias ruled a free Judah.

It's time to stop and look around at the rest of the world to see what's happening. Anything new, interesting, or mind-boggling? As we've seen, the Middle East had a constant parade of new empires marching into Jerusalem and taking over. It gets kind of confusing trying to figure out who's in charge. Was the rest of the world having the same kinds of problems?

The Wall!

China was having a hard time with invaders in their part of the world too. China was a powerful empire—with a royal emperor. But in the ancient world when a group of people became success-ful, wealthy, and pow-erful, that spelled trouble.

That trouble came in the form of a rough group of traveling tribes called the Xiongnu. Say it like this … Hsiung-nu. They kept riding in, raiding towns and villages, and riding right out again. What was China's answer to this problem? They made five hundred thousand soldiers and other common laborers build a huge earth, stone, and brick wall to keep the invaders out. This wall snaked along moun-tains, rivers, and valleys for fifteen hundred miles. It averaged from fifteen to thirty feet thick and was about twenty-five feet tall.

They say the Great Wall of China is the only man-made object you can see from the moon.

In the Americas!

In what is present-day Mexico, a mysterious city was being built about 200 B.C. Teotihuacan was the largest city in all of ancient North, Central, and South Americas with 100,000 to 200,000 people living there.

The people of Teotihuacan lived a peaceful life because we can find no signs of soldiers or military weapons. They built huge palaces and pyramids out of sun-dried bricks and stone. The Pyramid of the Sun would have been as large as the pyramids of Egypt. It was as tall as a twenty-story building.

Britain

Little is known about the early history of Britain. But we do know that by this time a strong group of wandering tribes called the Celts had crossed over from Europe to the islands of Britain. These tribes mingled with the people already living in villages there and brought their own language and ways of doing things. Each tribe or village of Celts had a chieftain or king and warriors to protect their group. They built protected forts on hilltops.

Meet Rome

About this same time, most of the known ancient world was falling into the hands of an empire with the most powerful army ever seen—the Romans! They went far into Europe, India, Egypt, and Britain. The huge Roman nation grew from small villages in what is now Italy to an empire of several million square miles. The Romans conquered and changed the world forever.

joke

Historian: **Doctor, I think I lost my memory.**
Doctor: **When did that happen?**
Historian: **When did what happen?**

CHINA
05 JAN 2002
IMMIGRATION OFFICER

Britain
IMMIGRATIONS
11 05 2003
PERMITTED ENTRY AS VISITOR ONLY

ROME
07 APR 2001
IMMIGRATION OFFICER

- The shortest war on record was fought between the United Kingdom and Zanzibar in 1896. It lasted only thirty-eight minutes.

- The Celt warriors had war chariots buried with them when they died.

DID YOU KNOW

Celtic grave with cross

Great Wall of China

Pyramid of the Sun at Teotihuacan

Ruins at Roman Forum

ARCTIC OCEAN

ATLANTIC OCEAN

PACIFIC OCEAN

PACIFIC OCEAN

INDIAN OCEAN

WELCOME TO ROME

When Jesus was born, the Roman Empire controlled most of the known world and, more importantly, Jerusalem. But who were these Romans who had everybody shaking in their sandals?

The city of Rome was the capital of the Roman Empire and the center of much of the civilized world. It was a city filled with great buildings, huge exotic markets, and foreigners from all over. Rome was filled with amazing builders, leaders, soldiers, engineers, inventors, and thinkers. How did the Romans get so smart? Simple! They took the best ideas and ways of doing things from all the countries they conquered and made them better. They would take the best teachers, artists, inventors, and athletes and bring them back to Rome to teach or train

young Romans. They collected wealth, people, and ideas.

The key to collecting this stuff was a loyal army. Whoever earned the respect of the Roman army ruled Rome. So the emperors of Rome were often great military leaders and always, always treated their soldiers well. A happy army worked hard to conquer more kingdoms to bring back more treasure and slaves for their emperor. Romans became extremely wealthy and extremely good at keeping their empire under control.

This wealth and power made the Romans a vain, self-important, and selfish people. They showed little mercy to the people they conquered. In fact, Rome was built on slave labor. At one point, there were more slaves in Rome than citizens.

joke

Why did the Romans build straight roads?

So their soldiers didn't go around the bend!

Roman Empire – 0 A.D.

Many Romans lived a lazy, comfortable life with slaves doing the daily chores and hard work. This left them free to design buildings, create art, and do other things they enjoyed. A lot of Romans lived in expensive homes, ate fine foods, and had time to enjoy themselves.

But the Romans considered sympathy a weakness. Murder and treacherous plots against one another were common practice—even among family members.

Show-Business Roman Style

The Romans loved to be entertained. They built the Colosseum, which could seat 50,000 people, and the Circus Maximus (like a huge racetrack), which could seat 260,000 people. Romans loved to watch violent sports in which men and women gladiators (specially trained fighters) battled each other or wild animals like

- The Romans invented concrete for their buildings and roads.
- Romans made great water systems or aqueducts to bring water into the city of Rome – about 200 million gallons every day.

DID YOU KNOW?

Colosseum

Aqueduct

bears, elephants, lions, bulls, hippopotamuses, rhinoceroses, and tigers. Usually they fought to the death. Naturally, they went through a lot of animals and people.

As many as five thousand animals were killed in a single day. The huge Roman empire was

able to keep the busy Colosseum in stock. But some animals were wiped out of certain areas, like the hippopotamus in Nubia.

Sometimes the Romans brought in slaves to fight. But oddly enough, young Romans volunteered by the thousands to become gladiators, because if they won their contests, they could become famous like movie stars today.

Roads

They used to say "all roads lead to Rome," which was kind of true. The Romans were the best road builders in the world. They built roads to the most distant points of their empire. This made it easier for their huge armies to travel quickly. Parts of these roads still remain today.

In God's Holy Land far, far away from Rome, two priests both wanted to rule. They asked powerful Rome to come help settle the argument. The Roman General Pompey agreed to come help. Help? Some help! He made the land of the Hebrews part of the Roman Empire. And he wouldn't leave. With help like that, who needs enemies? The Romans were in Jerusalem to stay.

During this time God sent his only son to Earth on a special mission. Jesus' mission was to redeem humankind from Adam and Eve's sin, so we could become God's children again—free of sin!

Did Jesus come with an army of angels ready to charge in and change the world? Although that sounds exciting, that wasn't God's plan. His plan began quietly in a little hick town in the backwoods—Bethlehem.

Bethlehem

Remember King David's small hometown called Bethlehem? In that same little town, a new king was born to a young woman named Mary. God had chosen Mary to be the mother of his son, and she agreed. She was told to name her son Jesus. Joseph, her future husband, also understood how special this new baby was, and he was ready to help raise Jesus as best he could. So in a simple stable in Bethlehem, God's son was born.

Herod on the Hunt

King Herod the Great was always suspicious because he felt unpopular and disliked. He thought everybody was planning to get rid of him. Hmm, maybe they were!

Anyway, Herod got really uptight when he heard a new king was born in Bethlehem. There was only going to be one king around here and that was Herod! So Herod ordered the murder of all the babies in Bethlehem. But an angel warned Mary and Joseph, and they escaped into Egypt with Jesus.

Nazareth

When King Herod the Great died, it was finally safe to go home, so Joseph brought his family back to the Holy Land to live in the town of Nazareth. It was a sleepy little hillside town fourteen miles

Joseph and Mary's Journeys

GALILEE
Nazareth
Sea of Galilee
Jordan River
THE GREAT SEA
(MEDITERRANEAN SEA)
Jerusalem
JUDEA
Gaza
Bethlehem
Dead Sea

0 20 40 miles
0 20 40 kilometers

Red Sea

SINAI

EXP. 14 FEB 2009

PERMITTED ENTRY AS VISITOR ONLY

NAZARETH

from the Sea of Galilee, which is actually a large inland lake in the northern part of the Holy land. About fifteen to twenty thousand people lived in Nazareth.

As a boy, Jesus spent his days with the other village boys in the synagogue, learning about the Bible. At home he probably trained to be a carpenter like Joseph.

John the Baptist

Let's flash ahead eighteen years, then hike around the wild and incredibly hot desert west of the Dead Sea. You just might find someone interesting there.

God had a really important plan for a man called John the Baptist. From a very early age, John had totally dedicated himself to God. He lived alone in the desert, eating only what he could find: things like wild honey and locust. That's right! Big, hopping bugs!

joke

How do you get a locust to roll over?

Tilt your plate.

Alone, John spent important time praying and studying God's Word. He often went to the Jordan River and preached to the large and curious crowds that came to hear him. He was the talk of the kingdom: who was this guy standing knee-deep in river water?

He urged people to tell God they were sorry for their sins. He wanted them to change their hearts and change their ways and to show this new life for God by being baptized in front of everybody. But most importantly, John told people that someone very special was coming who would change the world forever. Sending John was God's way of telling people that Jesus was here and amazing things were going to happen.

Dead Sea and Desert

Nazareth

Jesus was only thirty years old when he started traveling through villages and cities doing amazing things like healing the sick, raising the dead, and feeding the hungry. Let's hit the trail and look at some of those spots he visited to discover exactly what happened there.

Jordan River

The Jordan River flows 104 miles from Banias in the north down through Lake Huleh and the Sea of Galilee on its way to the Dead Sea. One day John was baptizing people in the river when Jesus came and asked to be baptized as well. Jesus wanted to do everything according to his Father's will and to set an example for others by being baptized. John agreed. God was very pleased, and this was just the right start for Jesus' ministry.

joke

What do you call a fisherman swimming in the Sea of Galilee?

Bob.

Mountain of Quarantania

After his baptism, Jesus went alone out into the wilderness. He didn't eat at all for forty days so that he could spend all his time and energy thinking about God. Satan came to tempt Jesus to do wrong things, but failed big time. Many people think Jesus was tempted while on Mount Quarantania— a lonely thirteen-hundred-foot-high cliff overlooking Jericho.

Capernaum

Capernaum was a busy fishing village on the northwestern shore of the Sea of Galilee. Jesus spent a lot of time there and often taught in the synagogue. Jesus did one of his first recorded miracles in Capernaum, healing Peter's sick mother-in-law. All that's left of Capernaum today is ten acres of ruins. Archaeologists have unearthed many of the village homes and streets.

Galilee

For two years Jesus traveled the highlands and farming valleys of the northern district of Galilee. He taught and did many amazing miracles there. He even fed five thousand people from one boy's small lunch of fish and bread.

Sea of Galilee

One night the disciples were sailing across the Sea of Galilee to a fishing town called Bethsaida, the hometown of Peter, Andrew, and Philip, when a huge storm suddenly came up. The waves crashed against the boat, terrifying the disciples. Even though they were in the middle of the lake, Jesus walked across the water to get to them. Peter also tried to walk on the water toward Jesus, but his faith just wasn't up to the task. He started to sink and called out for Jesus to help. Jesus helped Peter back into the boat and commanded the storm to be still.

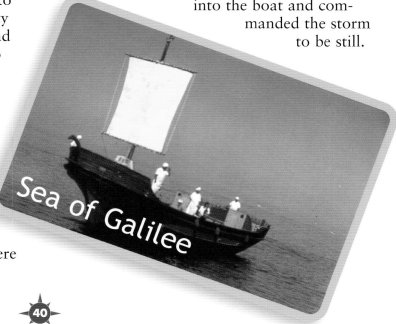

Sea of Galilee

International transportation artery
Regional roadway

THE GREAT SEA
(MEDITERRANEAN SEA)

▲ Mt. Hermon

Tyre

PHOENICIA

Transfiguration?
(possible site)

Caesarea Philippi

Heals Canaanite
woman's daughter

Predicts his
death

Sermon on
the Mount?

Heals the centurion's servant,
a paralytic, and Peter's
mother-in-law; restores
Jairus's daughter to life

Korazin

Heals blind Man;
feeds 5,000?

Ptolemais
(Acco)

Turns water
into wine

Bethsaida
Capernaum

Heals man
with demons
(Mk 5:1; Lk 8:26)

Cana

GALILEE

Magdala

Sea
of
Galilee

Khersa
(Gergesa?)

Walks on water;
quiets storm

Transfiguration?
(traditional site)

Tiberias

Nazareth

Mt.
Tabor

Yarmuk R.

Spends boyhood

Nain

Gadara

Heals men
with demons
(Mt 8:28)

Restores widow's
son to life

Caesarea
(Strato's Tower)

Bethany beyond
Jordan?

DECAPOLIS

Baptism
(possible site)

Salim?

SAMARIA

Jordan R.

Gerasa

Talks with
woman
at well

Sychar

Jabbok R.

Mt. Gerizim

Raises Lazarus from dead;
anointed in Simon the
Leper's house

PEREA

Tempted?

Ascends
into heaven

Baptism
(traditional site)

Clears
temple

Jericho

Emmaus?

▲ Mt. of Olives

Bethany beyond Jordan?

Bethany
Jerusalem

Appears to two
after resurrection

Heals blind Bartimaeus;
calls Zacchaeus down
from tree

Bethlehem

Birth

JUDEA

Salt
Sea

Crucifixion and
resurrection

Machaerus

Gadara

About six miles from the Sea of Galilee on top of a mountain was the city of Gadara. While there Jesus encountered two men who were possessed by as many as six thousand demons. Jesus told the demons to leave the men, and they obeyed. The demons went to live in a herd of two thousand pigs instead. The impressive ruins of Gadara surround the modern village of Um-Keis.

Gadara Ruins

Jericho

A new city of Jericho was built a little bit south of the ruins of ancient Jericho. It was also a beautiful city with many palm trees. One day as Jesus and a large crowd were entering the city, a blind man sitting beside the road heard who was approaching and called to Jesus. Jesus asked him what he wanted. The blind man said he wanted to see again. Jesus healed him, and instantly, the man's sight was restored. Talk about an eye-opener!

Don't forget there are many more interesting spots Jesus visited, so check out the action in the Bible.

EXP. 20 APR 2002

PERMITTED ENTRY AS VISITOR ONLY

JERICHO

Jericho

- There are four books in the Bible that tell about Jesus' life. They are called the Gospels. The writers of these books were Matthew, a tax collector; Luke, a doctor; John, a fisherman; and Mark.

- We don't know what Jesus looked like. There is no description of Jesus' appearance in any of the Gospels.

- Thirty to fifty parables or stories told by Jesus are recorded in the Gospels to help us understand God better.

DID YOU KNOW?

Jesus had spent three years on the road, teaching and ministering to people, but he knew he must die to free humankind from sin. He faced his death knowing that it was part of God's plan. Let's look at what Jesus did during his last week on earth.

Bethany

On Friday Jesus arrived in the picture-perfect village of Bethany, which was only two miles from Jerusalem. Lazarus, a good friend of Jesus, was giving a dinner to honor him … and for good reason! Just the month before, Jesus had raised Lazarus from the dead. On Saturday Jesus rested.

Jerusalem

On Sunday Jesus entered the great city of Jerusalem riding a young donkey. The excited crowd ran out to meet him, waving palm branches and shouting, "Hosanna! Blessed is he who comes in the name of the Lord! Blessed is the King of Israel!" (See John 12:13.) Jesus was extremely popular and loved by the people.

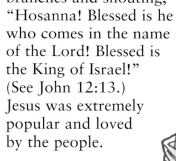

Trouble in the Temple

On Monday Jesus entered the temple at Jerusalem and was shocked and saddened by what he saw. In what should have been the holiest place in the world, people were selling animals. What was even worse, they were charging a hefty fee to exchange foreign money with visitors. Jesus got angry and chased the merchants out of the temple!

Temple Is for Teaching

The next day Jesus returned to the temple courts to teach the people. He told parables or stories explaining more about God's will and love.

Rest?

On Wednesday it's possible Jesus left the busy city to relax with his friends in Bethany again.

Last Supper

On Thursday evening Jesus and his students shared their Passover meal in the upper room of a house in the city of Jerusalem, perhaps Mark's mother's house. Jesus shared unleavened bread and ceremonial wine with his friends and asked that each time they did this to remember him. Then he told the disciples about his coming death.

The Garden

Later that evening Jesus went to pray in the quiet Garden of Gethsemane just outside the city of Jerusalem. The garden may have been at the foot of a small mountain covered in olive tree orchards—the Mount of Olives. Judas led the soldiers there, and Jesus was arrested.

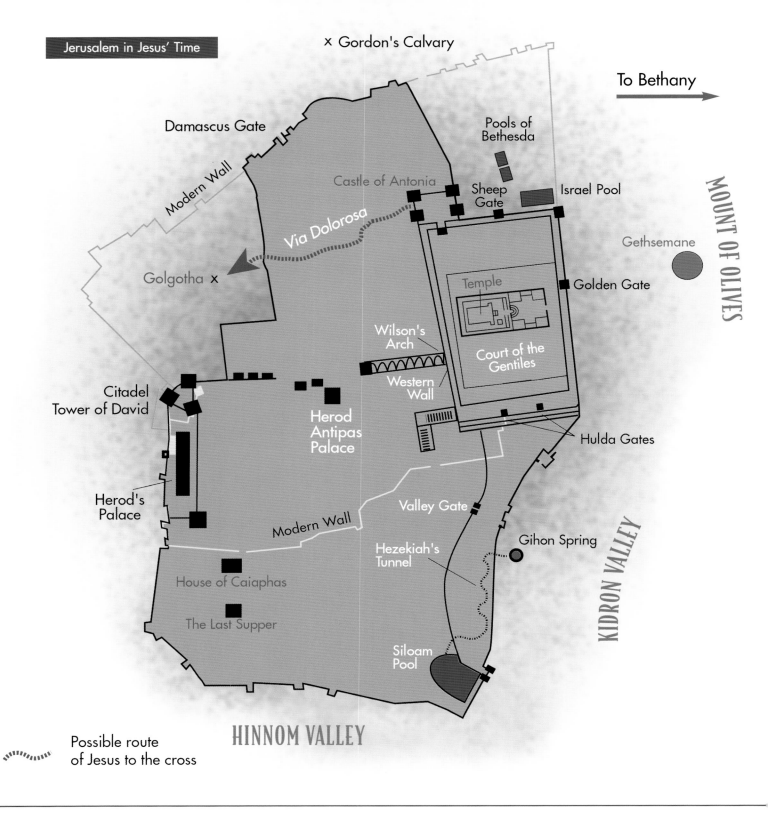

Jerusalem in Jesus' Time

Gordon's Calvary ✗

To Bethany →

Damascus Gate

Pools of Bethesda

Castle of Antonia

Sheep Gate

Israel Pool

MOUNT OF OLIVES

Gethsemane

Via Dolorosa

Modern Wall

Golgotha ✗

Temple

Golden Gate

Wilson's Arch

Court of the Gentiles

Western Wall

Citadel Tower of David

Herod Antipas Palace

Hulda Gates

Herod's Palace

Modern Wall

Valley Gate

Gihon Spring

KIDRON VALLEY

Hezekiah's Tunnel

House of Caiaphas

The Last Supper

Siloam Pool

HINNOM VALLEY

 Possible route of Jesus to the cross

Friday

Jesus arrives in Bethany and eats dinner with Lazarus.

Saturday

Jesus rests.

Sunday

Jesus enters the city of Jerusalem riding on a donkey.

Monday

Jesus throws merchants out of the temple.

House of Caiaphas

Jesus was taken to the house of the high priest Caiaphas in the city of Jerusalem. Jesus was questioned and sentenced to death. But they still needed the Roman government to approve.

The Castle of Antonia

On Friday Jesus was taken to the Castle of Antonia, a strong fortress near the temple, to meet the Roman in charge of Judea—Pontius Pilate. Pilate, wanting to avoid this Jewish problem, sent Jesus to see King Herod, who was at one of his city palaces celebrating the Passover. Herod laughed and sent him back to Pilate. Pilate had Jesus whipped, but the Jewish leaders wanted Jesus dead. Pilate finally agreed. The Roman army destroyed the Castle of Antonia along with the temple in A.D. 70.

Golgotha

Jesus was led through the streets of the city to an area outside the city walls called Golgotha (the skull). Researchers have identified two possible sites: one in the church of the Holy Sepulchur and the other known as Gordon's calvary. There Jesus was crucified along with two other men. This was a long, painful way to die.

The Tomb

The people who loved Jesus took his body and laid it in a tomb. There are two possible spots for the location of the tomb. Both are not far from the Damascus Gate, which is one of the two major entrances to the city.

- A tomb was either a natural cave or a small room dug into the side of stone cliffs. A boulder was usually fitted into the doorway to keep wild animals out.

DID YOU KNOW

Which is the right tomb? That's a good question! We aren't sure. Today thousands of tourists still visit Jerusalem and the tomb sites every year.

The Tomb

---

uesday

sus teaches in the mple.

Wednesday

Jesus rests?

Thursday

Jesus eats dinner with the twelve disciples.

Jesus prays in the Garden of Gethsemane and is arrested.

Friday

Jesus is crucified.

A completely innocent Jesus had allowed himself to die so he could take on himself all the sins of humankind. That was part of God's plan to correct the sin of Adam and Eve. But was that the end? Although all the details aren't certain, a comparison of all four Gospels leads us to think that the following is what happened that morning three days later.

The Tomb

In the early morning a good friend of Jesus named Mary Magdalene and some other women walked from Bethany to visit the tomb. Mary arrived at the tomb first and found it empty. Alarmed, she quickly ran to John's house not far away.

Meanwhile, the other group of women arrived at the tomb, but this time an angel told them that Jesus had risen from the dead. They ran to tell the others.

John, Peter, and Mary returned to the empty tomb. John was excited that his teacher had risen, but Peter was uncertain about what had really happened. They left, leaving a crying Mary behind. She was the first person Jesus showed himself to after rising from the dead. Mary was amazed and overjoyed!

Emmaus

That afternoon two of Jesus' disciples were walking the seven-mile journey from Jerusalem to a village called Emmaus. Jesus joined them on the road and talked with them. At first they did not recognize him, but later they realized who he was. They hurried back to Jerusalem to let everyone know.

Jerusalem

That night ten of the eleven remaining disciples met together to talk about the amazing things that were happening. Jesus was alive! In the middle of their conversation, Jesus appeared. He talked with them and ate with them. He explained to them what the Bible said about what had happened and God's awesome plan.

Sea of Galilee

Some of the disciples decided to take a boat out on the Sea of Galilee and fish. All night they didn't catch a thing. In the morning a man waved to them and encouraged them to throw their nets in again. What a haul! Now there were so many fish they couldn't pull the net into the boat. Peter realized it was Jesus and was so excited he jumped into the

joke

What do Bible researchers talk about when they get together?

Old times.

- The Bible records thirty-three of Jesus' amazing miracles.

- For forty days after his resurrection, Jesus visited and spoke with people.

- The disciples at the Sea of Galilee pulled out 153 large fish from their nets when Jesus appeared to them.

- One of the fastest fish in the world is the cosmopolitan sailfish. At 68 mph, it swims faster than a cheetah, which runs at 60 mph.

DID YOU KNOW?

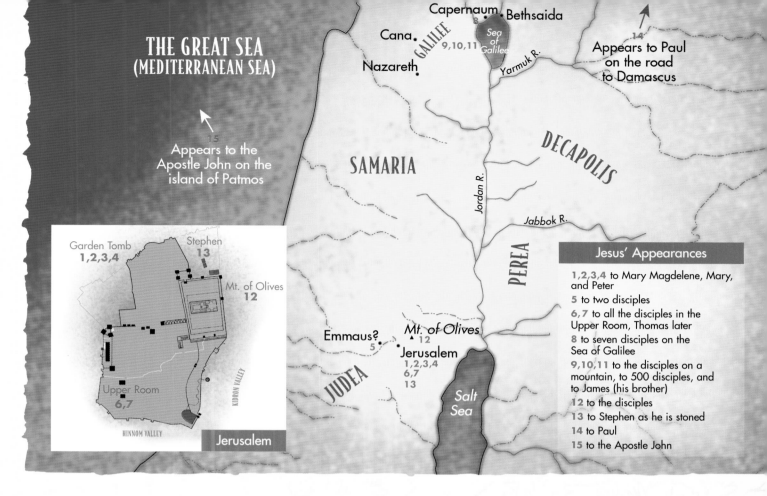

THE GREAT SEA
(MEDITERRANEAN SEA)

15
Appears to the
Apostle John on the
island of Patmos

Capernaum • Bethsaida
Cana
GALILEE
9,10,11
Sea
of
Galilee
Nazareth
Yarmuk R.

14
Appears to Paul
on the road
to Damascus

SAMARIA

DECAPOLIS

Jordan R.

Jabbok R.

PEREA

Jesus' Appearances

1,2,3,4 to Mary Magdelene, Mary, and Peter

5 to two disciples

6,7 to all the disciples in the Upper Room, Thomas later

8 to seven disciples on the Sea of Galilee

9,10,11 to the disciples on a mountain, to 500 disciples, and to James (his brother)

12 to the disciples

13 to Stephen as he is stoned

14 to Paul

15 to the Apostle John

Emmaus?
5
Mt. of Olives
12
Jerusalem
1,2,3,4
6,7
13

JUDEA

Salt
Sea

Jerusalem (inset):

Garden Tomb
1,2,3,4

Stephen
13

Mt. of Olives
12

Upper Room
6,7

KIDRON VALLEY

HINNOM VALLEY

Jerusalem

---

water and swam to shore. Then Jesus had breakfast with his friends.

Mountain

On a mountain in Galilee, Jesus reassured his friends and disciples that he would always be with them. He told them to go and baptize people from all nations in the name of the Father, the Son, and the Holy Spirit. The disciples had a lifetime job of teaching the world all that Jesus had taught them.

Bethany

The disciples journeyed with Jesus to a spot near Bethany, perhaps the quiet Mount of Olives. Jesus once again talked with his friends about their future. Jesus blessed his friends, then rose up into the sky until he disappeared in the clouds.

Jesus had done all the things that his Father in heaven had wanted him to do. He had defeated Satan, paid for humankind's sin, and taught us how to please God.

Mount of Olives

JUNE 20
2010

BETHANY

IMMIGRATION
ADMISSIONS

It must have been both an exciting and confusing time for Jesus' friends after he left. There was so much to do! How could they do it all without his help? But Jesus did promise them help! If we check back in with the disciples ten days after Jesus rose into the sky, we'll see some amazing things.

Pentecost

Jesus told his disciples to stay in Jerusalem and wait for the helpful gift of the Holy Spirit from his heavenly Father. The disciples were together in a room (perhaps at Mark's mother's house again) when suddenly a strong wind filled the entire house. They saw something that looked like tongues of fire landing on each of them. Then each person was filled with God's gift of the Holy Spirit. The Holy Spirit would give each of them the right words, miracles, and boldness to tell friends and enemies about Jesus.

This all happened during the Jewish celebration of the harvest (Pentecost). Many Jews from all over the ancient world had come to the city to celebrate. At least fifteen nations were represented, and they came to listen to Jesus' disciples speak. Then the most amazing thing happened! Because of the power of the Holy Spirit, each disciple was able to speak to the visitors in their own language even if they had never spoken it before. Remember, God had separated the people at the Tower of Babel, and now he was joining them together again with the Holy Spirit. There was no longer a language barrier to stop the spread of the Gospel.

God had used the nation of Israel as the starting point of bringing people together in their belief in his son Jesus. It didn't matter if you were Jewish or not. Jesus' sacrifice, love, and salvation was for everybody in the world who believed in him. Jesus had opened the door, and he was the way everyone would return to the heavenly Father. Now that's something to talk about!

Not Wanted

Over the next few months the disciples worked hard telling everybody about Jesus. Already there were more than three thousand believers! The Jewish religious leaders were not at all happy that people still believed in Jesus. Frustrated and angry, they treated members of the early church very badly. Men and women were arrested, beaten, and sometimes killed!

joke

First Roman soldier:
What time is it?

Second Roman soldier:
Oh, about XX past VII.

Samaria

EXP.
28 FEB
2008

PERMITTED
ENTRY AS
VISITOR ONLY

MARIA

Caesarea

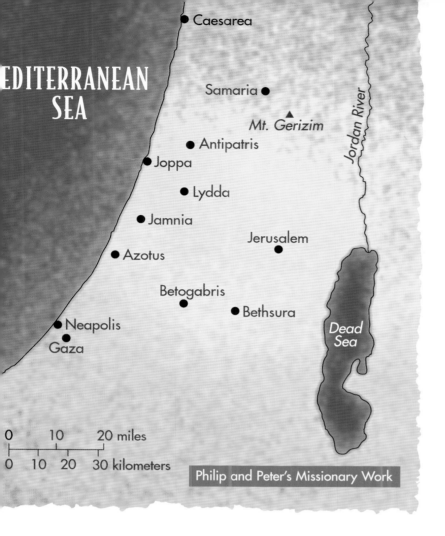

Philip and Peter's Missionary Work

Peter. Cornelius and his family believed and were baptized. They were the first non-Jews to join the church.

Samaria

Many foreigners had settled in Samaria and married the Jews who lived there. So some of the neighboring areas felt the Samaritans weren't really proper Jews. This caused some hard feelings, but Philip reached out to them with the love of Jesus, and many came to believe!

Caesarea

A seaside town on the shores of the Mediterranean called Caesarea was the command center for the Roman soldiers. It was only about seventy miles from Jerusalem. A Roman centurion or commander named Cornelius sent for

CAESAREA
06 mar 2011
PERMITTED ENTRY
AS VISITOR ONLY

- A Roman centurion would have a hundred soldiers under his command.

- The Roman roads helped spread the news of Jesus farther and faster.

- Which book in the world has sold the most copies? The Bible, with more than 2.5 billion copies.

THE FIRST STEP IS THE MOST IMPORTANT

The man who really logged the miles when it came to spreading the Good News was a guy named Paul. Nope, he wasn't one of the twelve original disciples. In fact, he was one of the bad guys who went after the early church to wipe it out. Paul's life journey is one of the best examples of how God can change your heart.

EXP.
28 SEP
2009

PERMITTED
ENTRY AS
VISITOR ONLY
ANTIOCH

TARSUS
03 APR 1998
PERMITTED
ENTRY AS
VISITOR
ONLY

He hated all Christians because he thought they dishonored God and caused problems for the Jews. Paul terrorized the Christians in Jerusalem by arresting and beating them. Many fled, but Paul planned to hunt them down in the city of Damascus.

Damascus

Damascus is about 133 miles from Jerusalem, and on Paul's journey there, Jesus appeared to him. As a result, Paul became a Christian! He was one of the most outgoing preachers in the early church.

Tarsus

Paul was born in the wealthy Greek city of Tarsus on the river Cydnus along the coast of the Mediterranean.

Paul's Missionary Journeys

First Missionary Journey (A.D. 46–48)
Second Missionary Journey (A.D. 49–52)
Third Missionary Journey (A.D. 53–57)
Trip to Rome (A.D. 59–60)

0   100   200 mi.
0 100 200 300 km.

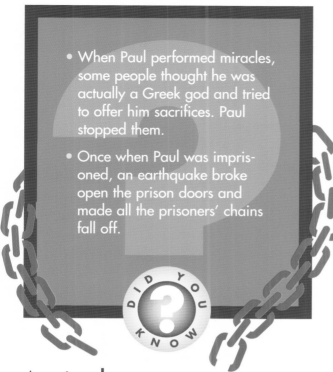

- When Paul performed miracles, some people thought he was actually a Greek god and tried to offer him sacrifices. Paul stopped them.

- Once when Paul was imprisoned, an earthquake broke open the prison doors and made all the prisoners' chains fall off.

DID YOU KNOW ?

Rome

A very, very evil man named Nero was emperor of Rome by this time, and he set out to destroy the Christians in his empire. He gathered up Christian men, women, and children and had them killed in horrible ways for sport in the great Colosseum of Rome. Paul was arrested and taken to Rome to stand trial before Nero. Sadly, Paul was put to death and his journeys were finally over. But his voice still teaches us through the letters he wrote to the many churches that he helped build all across the Roman Empire. You'll find those letters in the New Testament.

joke

Why did Paul travel so much?

Because he was roamin'!

Antioch

A few years later Paul traveled to the church in Antioch, the Roman capital in Syria. Paul became an important member of the church, but he was eager to spread the news of Jesus to all the world.

Paul went on four long road trips and traveled for many years by land and ship. Often he would go to the synagogues to preach. He would perform healings and other miracles, and many people became believers. But more often than not, angry religious leaders would soon run Paul out of town.

Caesarea

Paul had returned to Jerusalem but was almost murdered by an angry mob at the temple. The good news—a Roman officer rescued him. The bad news—he was taken to Caesarea and put into prison for two years. Paul was a prisoner in the palace of Felix, the Roman governor. They often spoke together. Many of the Roman soldiers who guarded Paul became believers. When Paul was released—you guessed it—he was on the road again preaching.

Damascus

Paul's Prison

ROM
07 APR 2

IMMIGRAT
OFFICE

It became illegal to be a Christian in the Roman Empire about the year A.D. 250. If you were discovered, you either had to deny your faith in Jesus or be killed. Many, many Christians chose death or a short, hard life as a slave.

The Romans may have hated the Christians, but they admired their bravery. Despite all the bad things that happened, not even Rome could stop Jesus' words from spreading like wildfire. In fact, 15 percent of the population of the empire became Christians! That's about fifty to seventy-five million people!

Constantine

In A.D. 312 a Roman emperor by the name of Constantine came to power. He was getting ready to fight an important battle when God sent him a vision of the cross with these words written on it: "In this sign, conquer." He won his battle and became the first Christian Roman emperor. Christianity was soon a legal and official religion of the Roman Empire. Way to go, Constantine!

Trouble in the Church

Constantine took the scattered communities of believers and made them a government-supported religion. He made the church a part of the government and kicked off what we now

Roman Empire at it's Greatest Extent

GERMAN SEA

BRITAIN

London

ATLANTIC OCEAN

Cologna
Rhine R.
Mainz
GERMANY

Vistula R.

Volga R.

Loire R.

GAUL

Dnieper R.

SARMATIA

Lyons
Rhône R.

ALPS

Po R.

Danube R.

ILLYRICUM

DACIA

CAUCASUS MTS.

CASPIAN SEA

Tagus R.

SPAIN

CORSICA

Rome
ITALY

Solona

ADRIATIC SEA

MOESIA

BLACK SEA

Cyrus R.

ARMENIA

SARDINIA

TYRRHENIAN SEA

Puteoli

MACEDONIA
Thessalonica

THRACE
Philippi

AEGEAN SEA
MYSIA
Pergamum

Byzantium

BITHYNIA & PONTUS

GALATIA

PHRYGIA

CAPPADOCIA

Edessa

Euphrates R.

MESOPOTAMIA

PARTHIA

Tigris R.

MAURETANIA

Carthage

SICILY
Syracuse

ACHAIA
Corinth
Athens

Ephesus
Derbe

CILICIA
Tarsus

Antioch

SYRIA

Dura-Europos

AFRICA

MEDITERRANEAN SEA

CRETE

CYPRUS

Sidon
Tyre
JUDEA
Pella

Damascus

NABATEA

ARABIAN DESERT

Cyrene

Jerusalem

Alexandria

0   200   400   600 mi.
0   200   400   600   800 km.

CYRENE

Memphis

Nile R.

Antinoe

EGYPT

RED SEA

know as the Holy Roman Catholic Church. The Christian church was soon involved in upholding the law and governing and managing cities and even kingdoms. That move would make the church a very powerful force in the world for hundreds of years to follow.

This was both a good thing and a bad thing. Many evil men joined the church just to gain power over people and enjoy the wealth that came with that power. But even though many bad things were done in the name of the church, there were also many good things done by good people.

Trouble in Rome

The Roman Empire was in big trouble by A.D. 455. After ruling the world for hundreds of years and using slaves to do all their work, the Romans had become lazy. The once proud Roman army was weak. Rough gangs of Germanic tribes from Europe attacked the empire until finally they captured Rome.

Rome's strict control and "law and order" that had once made the empire a safe place to live was gone. Soon all the roads, water systems, and cities that made the Roman Empire great disappeared. The world was entering a period commonly known as the Dark or Middle Ages.

Catacombs

ter for travelers. They were a safe place in a dangerous world. They made life a lot better.

They also copied the ancient manuscripts or writings passed down from Jesus' disciples. They kept the books of the Bible safe for the future. Most importantly, the people's faith in Jesus gave different villages and kingdoms something in common. They were all brothers and sisters in Christ!

The Church Did Some Good!

The church was the light in that dark time. Groups of Christians formed their own communities or monasteries where they served God and people. These Christian centers—some run by all women and some run by all men—started schools, built roads, farmed, fed the poor, cared for the sick, and provided shel-

Holy Roman Empire

Over hundreds of years little kings fought over land and power. But in A.D. 768 one strong leader named Charlemagne pulled it all together and made a new powerful Christian empire called the Holy Roman Empire. And his empire ruled most of Christian Europe. That was the start of big things for the church.

EXPLORING THE YEAR 1000!

The year 1000 was a busy time for the entire world. People were exploring new lands, agreeing on some things, and doing a whole lot of disagreeing on most things! There were also famines and terrible plagues.

Islam

A new religion was growing and spreading fast. In Arabia a man named Mohammed felt Christians were worshipping three gods in God the Father, Jesus Christ, and the Holy Spirit. So Mohammed started a religion based on the Old Testament of the Bible. He wanted to worship only one god named Allah. He believed Jesus was only a great teacher and prophet.

People from all over Arabia, Spain, North Africa, and India accepted this new religion, called Islam. Much of the world divided into kingdoms that were Muslim or Islamic and kingdoms that were Christian.

It wouldn't be long before these two religions started a two-hundred-year-old battle (The Crusades) that would change history. The Christian kingdoms got together and decided to free the Holy Land from the powers of Islam. It just happened that they also wanted to gain control of the rich trade routes while they were there. Hmmm.

Africa

Africa was the home of some very powerful kingdoms. The kingdom of Ghana in West Africa traded in gold, ivory, tools, leather, jewelry, and slaves with southern Africa, Arabia, and Europe. Foreign traders and merchants returned home awed by the wealth of Africa.

North America

Native Americans built large villages in the southwest of North America around where Arizona and New Mexico are today. These people lived a good life, farming corn, beans, squash, and cotton, as well as raising turkeys for food. They built large apartment-like buildings called pueblos. Archaeologists have found one pueblo that contained eight hundred rooms and think it may have housed as many as a thousand people.

Meanwhile, way up north, a sailor named Leif Ericson (or "Lucky" Leif to his friends) sailed from a village in Greenland to the shores of North America—researchers think somewhere between Newfoundland and New England. He was one of the first Europeans to explore North America.

Japan

Japan carefully watched the empires of China and in many ways tried to copy them. A leader named Michinaga took control of the Japanese empire and began to make Japan … well … more Japanese and less Chinese. But Japan broke down into a kingdom filled with small but powerful lords and their warriors, who controlled property and villages. There were constant small battles between competing lords over land and power.

joke

Why was this time period in history called the Dark Ages?

Because there were so many knights!

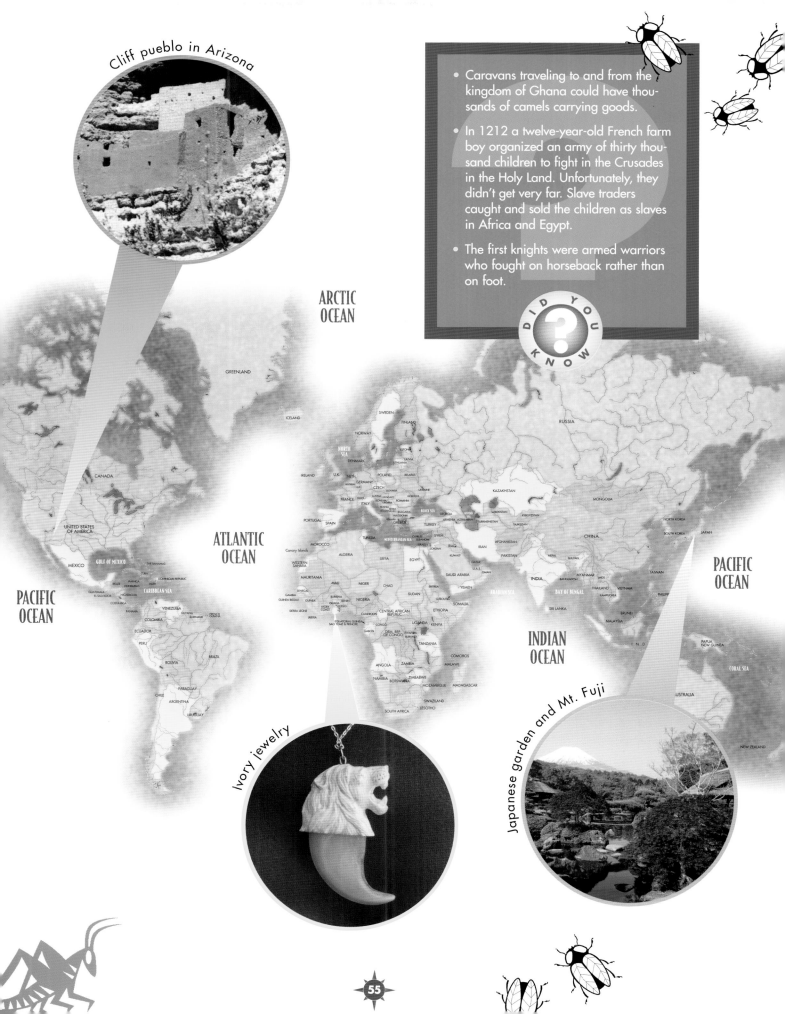

Cliff pueblo in Arizona

ARCTIC OCEAN

ATLANTIC OCEAN

PACIFIC OCEAN

PACIFIC OCEAN

INDIAN OCEAN

GREENLAND
ICELAND
SWEDEN
FINLAND
NORWAY
RUSSIA
NORTH SEA
DENMARK
ESTONIA
LATVIA
IRELAND
U.K.
NETH.
LITHUANIA
BELARUS
BELGIUM
GERMANY
POLAND
LUX.
CZECH
SLOVAKIA
UKRAINE
KAZAKHSTAN
MONGOLIA
FRANCE
SWITZ.
AUSTRIA
HUNGARY
MOLDOVA
ROMANIA
ITALY
SLOVENIA
CROATIA
BOSNIA
BLACK SEA
GEORGIA
ARMENIA
AZERBAIJAN
UZBEKISTAN
KYRGYZSTAN
NORTH KOREA
PORTUGAL
SPAIN
GREECE
TURKEY
TURKMENISTAN
TAJIKISTAN
CHINA
SOUTH KOREA
JAPAN
CANADA
BULGARIA
MACEDONIA
CYPRUS
LEBANON
SYRIA
IRAQ
IRAN
AFGHANISTAN
MOROCCO
MEDITERRANEAN SEA
ISRAEL
JORDAN
KUWAIT
PAKISTAN
NEPAL
BHUTAN
NORTH KOREA
UNITED STATES OF AMERICA
ALGERIA
LIBYA
EGYPT
SAUDI ARABIA
QATAR
U.A.E.
INDIA
BANGLADESH
MYANMAR
LAOS
TAIWAN
GULF OF MEXICO
WESTERN SAHARA
MAURITANIA
MALI
NIGER
CHAD
SUDAN
ERITREA
YEMEN
ARABIAN SEA
BAY OF BENGAL
THAILAND
VIETNAM
PHILIPPINES
MEXICO
THE BAHAMAS
CUBA
CANARY ISLANDS
SENEGAL
GAMBIA
BURKINA
DJIBOUTI
SRI LANKA
KAMPUCHEA
BRUNEI
JAMAICA
HAITI
DOMINICAN REPUBLIC
GUINEA BISSAU
GUINEA
GHANA
TOGO
NIGERIA
SOMALIA
MALAYSIA
GUATEMALA
BELIZE
HONDURAS
SIERRA LEONE
IVORY COAST
BENIN
CENTRAL AFRICAN REPUBLIC
ETHIOPIA
I N D O N E S I A
EL SALVADOR
NICARAGUA
CARIBBEAN SEA
LIBERIA
CAMEROON
UGANDA
KENYA
PAPUA NEW GUINEA
COSTA RICA
PANAMA
VENEZUELA
GUYANA
SURINAME
FRENCH GUIANA
EQUATORIAL GUINEA
SAO TOME & PRINCIPE
GABON
CONGO
DEM. REP. OF CONGO
RWANDA
BURUNDI
TANZANIA
CORAL SEA
COLOMBIA
ECUADOR
ANGOLA
ZAMBIA
COMOROS
MALAWI
AUSTRALIA
PERU
BRAZIL
BOLIVIA
NAMIBIA
ZIMBABWE
BOTSWANA
MOZAMBIQUE
MADAGASCAR
PARAGUAY
SWAZILAND
CHILE
ARGENTINA
SOUTH AFRICA
LESOTHO
NEW ZEALAND
URUGUAY

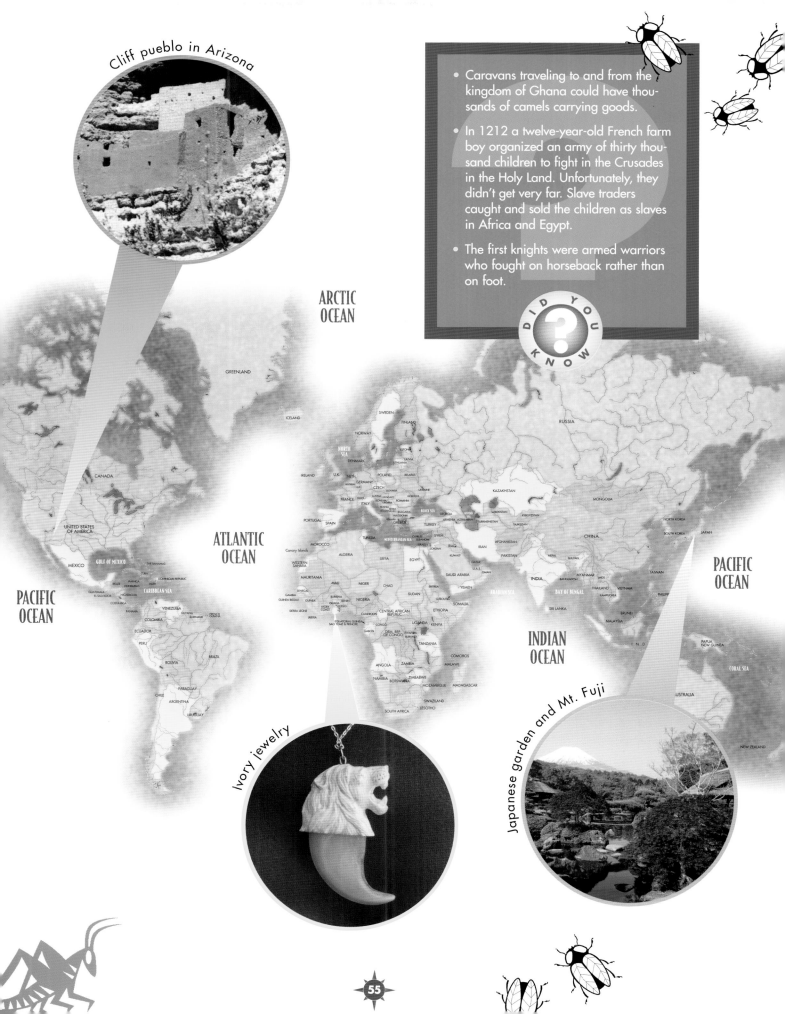
Ivory jewelry

Japanese garden and Mt. Fuji

Finally, the two-hundred-year war with Islam was over. The armies of Islam reclaimed Jerusalem, and the European Christians went home. The European Christian kingdoms were getting on with normal life and building big churches called cathedrals—sometimes dozens of them in one kingdom! In France alone 1,587 churches were built.

Stained-glass windows filled the churches with flashes of colorful sunlight. Often each window would be a scene from a Bible story. Because most people couldn't read, these windows helped them remember the Bible stories.

joke

How could a missionary go without sleep for seven days and not be tired?

She slept at night.

The Bible–Read All About It

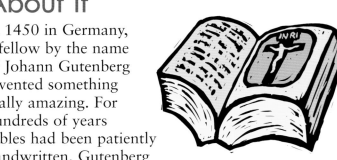

In 1450 in Germany, a fellow by the name of Johann Gutenberg invented something really amazing. For hundreds of years Bibles had been patiently handwritten. Gutenberg invented the first printing press with movable metal type. That was a big deal! The first book off the press was the Gutenberg Bible. Bibles could now be produced faster, easier, cheaper, and in multiple copies.

Then John Wycliffe of England sat down one day and decided that having the Bible written in Latin or Greek didn't do the ordinary person any good. Why? Because people couldn't read Latin or Greek! Most people relied on their priest or religious leaders to tell them what the Bible said. John Wycliffe and others translated the Bible into the languages that people did speak or read. Hey! Good idea, John!

Major Churches of Europe

Notre Dame Cathedral

Stained Glass

Leaving!

Because of all the fighting over church types, many European people decided to pack up and head off to quieter places where they could worship the way they wanted. Where did they go? By 1565 Christians looking for religious freedom settled North America, Africa, South America, and many other countries.

New Look At Teaching

A German named Martin Luther thought the Roman Catholic Church had missed a few important points. It was common practice for people to pay money, do good works, or go on long religious journeys to pay for their sins. These practices also helped the church raise money for building more churches. Martin Luther preached that God's loving and forgiving heart was the only thing that would free people of sin.

That idea set off a chain reaction of other Christians all over Europe saying similar things. Everybody wanted to start a church. Pretty soon there were Lutherans, Anglicans, Presbyterians, Methodists, Congregationalists, Dutch Reformed, Baptists, Quakers, and the list goes on. All this reformation or changing the way people conducted their churches went on for hundreds of years, from about 1300 to 1648.

But splitting the church into different denominations or types of churches didn't come easy. Kingdoms and rulers split over what type of church should be the spiritual ruling power. It got ugly, and wars sometimes broke out.

A Mission to Mission

New settlements or towns in these new lands became the launching point for missionaries to travel even further into the unexplored territory of South America, North America, Africa, and Asia. They wanted to reach new people with Christian teachings. They also set up schools and hospitals and in general tried to help out. These missionaries were carrying on Jesus' charge of bringing the Gospel to the entire world. There are many missionary societies or groups today that have been around for hundreds of years!

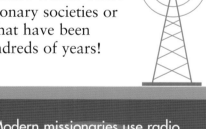

- Modern missionaries use radio, television, the Internet, and films to tell the world about the Good News. The first regular Christian radio broadcast took place in 1920 in Pittsburgh, Pennsylvania.

- The record holder for the world's largest church is the Yoido Full Gospel Church in Seoul, Korea, with 800,000 members! Better arrive early if you want a good seat!

DID YOU KNOW

THE WORLD TODAY!

Have you looked around to see what's happening in the world today? The world doesn't seem as large as it did long ago. We have super-fast jets and satellites that circle the earth and give us instant news day or night. But despite how close the world has become, we are still divided in what we believe and how we express our faith. That split happened long ago at the Tower of Babel. Ever since then people have had different ideas about God and religion. Let's take a look at these faiths and where they are on our global map today.

Christianity

What is found in the middle of both America and Australia?

The letter "r".

Paul would be happy to know that Christianity is the most widely scattered religion in the entire world. It is estimated that there are more than 1.7 billion Christians in the world today. That was God's plan all along!

Judaism

The Jewish faith or Judaism is a very old religion. Christians believe they have found the Messiah in Jesus Christ, while Jews are still waiting for him. The Jewish holy book is called the Torah, the first five books of what

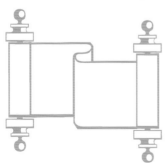

Christians call the Old Testament. There are synagogues in almost every part of the world and more than 12.8 million Jewish people in the world. About 3.9 million live in Israel.

Islam

The Islamic or Muslim faith still has a huge presence in our world today. One billion people worldwide follow the teachings of Mohammed and read their holy books called the Koran and Sunna. Islam is the main religion in many parts of Africa, the Middle East, and Central Asia. But it is also growing in India, Pakistan, Bangladesh, Indonesia, Malaysia, the Philippines, the United States, Canada, Europe, and China.

Hinduism

One of the world's oldest religions, Hinduism started in India about 1500 B.C. Most Hindus worship hundreds of different gods. Their holy writings are called the Vedas. There are more than 700 million Hindus worldwide. Most people in India are Hindu. But you will find Hinduism in areas of Africa, Asia, East Indies, and England.

Buddhism

Buddhism is another one of the world's major religions. It started in India and is based on the teachings of a man called Siddhartha Gautama, better known as Buddha or the Enlightened One. He lived more than

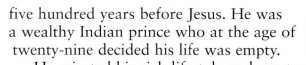

five hundred years before Jesus. He was a wealthy Indian prince who at the age of twenty-nine decided his life was empty. He rejected his rich lifestyle and went on a search for peace and the meaning of life.

There are between 150 to 300 million people in the world who follow the teachings of Buddha. Buddhism has a strong influence in India, Sri Lanka, Thailand, Cambodia, Myanmar, Laos, Japan, China, Taiwan, Tibet, Nepal, Mongolia, Korea, and Vietnam.

Taosim

Taoism is a Chinese way of thinking about life and faith. Taoists find instructions for life in writings called the Chuang-tzu. Taoism was the official religion of China but is frowned upon by the current Chinese government.

The Message

No matter where you live or what your background is, Jesus' message is for you. You don't have to be born Christian or live in a mostly Christian country either. The message is simple—Jesus died to free us all from sin. What you do with that message is simple too! Just believe in Jesus' love and salvation and learn how God wants you to live your life. That message is coming in loud and clear around the world!

- Otto Brechel of Mars, Pennsylvania, never missed a Sunday church service for eighty-eight years. That's 4,576 Sundays in a row!

DID YOU KNOW

THE FUTURE

It's easy to look back and study the past. It's just a matter of finding the pieces that were left behind and putting them back together. But what about the future? Can anybody know what's going to happen tomorrow or even a hundred years from now? Nope! Only God knows the future. But Jesus did talk to us about our future with God.

The Plan!

Jesus said some pretty important things about our future. First, he gave us a job to do, and that job didn't suddenly disappear when the disciples died. That job applies to us today. Jesus said, "All authority in heaven and on earth has been given to me. So you must go and make disciples of all nations. Baptize them in the name of the Father and of the Son and of the Holy Spirit. Teach them to obey everything I have commanded you. And you can be sure that I am always with you, to the very end" (Matthew 28:18-20).

That doesn't mean that all of us have to travel the world like Paul. It can mean just sharing our love for God with a friend and supporting others who translate and send Bibles around the world. We want to help people share the Gospel.

Next important thing to remember is this: Jesus is coming back. How do we know? The Bible tells us so!

Coming Back!

Jesus had done the seemingly impossible by taking our sins on himself and returning us to his Father free of sin. All of Satan's plans were destroyed. And Satan himself will be destroyed when Jesus returns again at the end of time. When will Jesus return? Nobody knows! In fact, "No one knows about that day or hour. Not even the angels in heaven know. The Son does not know. Only the Father knows" (Matthew 24:36).

Heaven

The Bible says that after the Second Coming of Jesus, God is going to do a little remodeling. We are going to get an all-new heaven and earth. And it's going to be great! Check out what the Bible says about heaven. "Now God makes his home with human beings. He will live with them. They will be his people. And God himself will be with them and be their God. He will wipe away every tear from their eyes. There will be no more death or sadness. There will be no more crying or pain. Things are no longer the way they used to be" (Revelation 21:3-4).

Being in heaven will be like your happiest moment multiplied by a zillion billion! Don't you just love surprises? God loves you! You can trust him with your future.

God gave us a wonderful world and universe to live in so that we would be happy. Because of Adam and Eve, we got detoured by sin and traveled through a lot of rough spots along the way. But Jesus is our signpost and way back home to the great life God had planned for us all along.

The Way

Jesus' death has opened the way for anyone who believes to go to heaven. He died for our sin so we wouldn't have to! But that doesn't give us an automatic ticket to heaven. We need to personally accept what Jesus did for us. When we do, God comes to live in us and to teach and care for us. Then we can do things God's way and live a good life. It's as simple as asking God's forgiveness for our sins and asking Jesus to be in our lives forever.

But each person has to make that choice. "Say with your mouth, 'Jesus is Lord.' Believe in your heart that God raised him from the dead. Then you will be saved" (Romans 10:9). It doesn't matter where you live. Your geography doesn't affect your decision. You are invited to take this step of faith wherever you are.

God's got one fantastic future just waiting for you. He's planned it from the beginning of time. You don't need a map to find God. Just pray and God will always find you. After all, he knows exactly where you are on his map!

Heaven

HEAVEN
??????????
IMMIGRATION
OFFICER:
GOD

MAP OF THE WORLD

ARCTIC OCEAN

GREENLAND

PACIFIC OCEAN

ATLANTIC OCEAN

ICELAND

IRELAND

PORTUGAL

MOROCCO

Canary Islands

WESTERN SAHARA

MAURITANIA

SENEGAL
GAMBIA
GUINEA BISSAU
GUINEA
SIERRA LEONE
LIBERIA

CANADA

UNITED STATES OF AMERICA

MEXICO

GULF OF MEXICO

THE BAHAMAS

Tropic of Cancer

CARIBBEAN SEA

DOMINICAN REPUBLIC
HAITI
JAMAICA
HONDURAS

GUATEMALA
EL SALVADOR
NICARAGUA
COSTA RICA
PANAMA

VENEZUELA
COLOMBIA
ECUADOR
PERU
GUYANA
SURINAME
FRENCH GUIANA

Equator

BRAZIL

BOLIVIA

PARAGUAY

CHILE

ARGENTINA

URUGUAY

Tropic of Capricorn

Barrow
Fort Yukon
Fairbanks
Anchorage
Cordova
Nome
Unalaska
Prince Rupert
Juneau
Bear Lake
Prince George
Kamloops
Seattle
Portland
Twin Falls
Reno
Oakland
San Francisco
Los Angeles
San Diego
Las Vegas
Phoenix
Tucson
Albuquerque
Denver
Kansas City
St. Louis
Memphis
Dallas
Houston
Birmingham
Atlanta
Charlotte
Washington D.C.
Baltimore
New York
Buffalo
Ottawa
Montreal
Chicago
Milwaukee
Minneapolis
Omaha
Scottsbluff
Grand Forks
Williston
Spokane
Butte
Provo
Port Radium
Fort Chipewyan
Fort McMurray
Dawson Creek
Grande Prairie
Red Deer
Calgary
Swift Current
Saskatoon
Prince Albert
Flin Flon
Thompson
Brandon
Baker Lake
Rankin Inlet
Churchill
Inukjuak
Moosonee
Timmins
Amos
Labrador City
Reykjavik
Dublin
Lisbon
Gibraltar
Santa Delgada
Nouakchott
Dakar
Banjul
Conakry
Freetown
Monrovia

Mexico City
Belize
BELIZE
Havana

Bogota
Quito
Tatara
Trujillo
Lima
La Paz
Sucre
Cuiaba
Goiania
Brasilia
Belo Horizonte
Campinas
Asuncion
Antofagasta
Santiago
Concepcion
Valdivia
Neuquen
Rosario
Buenos Aires
Montevideo
Comodoro Rivadavia
Port Stanley
Manaus
Belem
Porto Velho
Cachimbo
Sao Goncalo
Barreiras
Salvador
Recife
Curitiba
Georgetown
Paramaribo

Kidatlas
Copyright © 2002 by Lightwave Publishing Inc.

Requests for information should be addressed to:

Zonder**kidz**™

The children's group of Zondervan
Grand Rapids, Michigan 49530
www.zonderkidz.com

ISBN: 0-310-70059-0

Art direction by Jody Langley
Design by Lori Vezina
Printed in China

building Christian faith in families

A Lightwave Production
P.O. Box 160 Maple Ridge
B.C., Canada V2X 7G1
www.lightwavepublishing.com

02 03 04 05 06 07 / HK/ 10 9 8 7 6 5 4 3 2 1